The DNA of Financial Greatness

JUSTINE EHIWARIO

TABLE OF CONTENTS

SUMMARY

The DNA of Financial Greatness

The DNA of Financial Greatness is a transformative guide that equips individuals with the tools and strategies to achieve long-term wealth and financial freedom. In this insightful book, Justine Ehiwario delves into the core principles and methods used by successful people to generate, manage, and preserve wealth. Drawing from his own experiences and knowledge shared in his previous works, Justine provides a clear path for those determined to master their financial future.

The book simplifies the often complex process of wealth creation into practical, actionable steps, covering essential topics like financial literacy, smart investment practices, growing businesses, effective money management, and cultivating a wealth-focused mindset. Readers will discover how to accelerate their financial growth, embrace technology to their advantage, and take well-considered risks to maximize financial success.

A key focus of the book is on building lasting wealth for future generations and using financial success to make a positive impact. With real-life examples, valuable advice, and motivational stories, *The DNA of Financial Greatness* encourages readers to unlock their own financial potential, turning their aspirations into reality while building a secure, prosperous future.

Acknowledgments

First and foremost, I would like to express my deepest gratitude to God for His guidance, wisdom, and unwavering support throughout my journey. It is through His grace that I have been able to share my experiences and insights in this book.

To my family, thank you for your endless love, encouragement, and belief in me. Your support and understanding have been a constant source of strength, and this book is as much yours as it is mine.

A special thank you to those whose belief in my vision has inspired me every step of the way. Your wisdom and feedback have been invaluable.

To my mentors and teachers, both past and present, thank you for sharing your knowledge and perspectives. Your guidance has shaped my understanding of financial success and has influenced the ideas presented in this book.

I also want to express my heartfelt appreciation to my team and collaborators, whose dedication and hard work are the backbone of everything I do. This book would not have been possible without your contributions.

To my readers, thank you for trusting in my words. I am deeply grateful for the opportunity to share this journey with you, and I hope the lessons within these pages will serve as a catalyst for your own pursuit of financial greatness.

Finally, to anyone who has ever inspired me, supported me, or believed in me—this book is a reflection of all the wisdom, love, and hard work that surrounds me. Thank you for being a part of my story.

Whether you're just starting out or refining your financial strategies, this book offers the ultimate guide to attaining financial greatness and living a life of abundance.

With heartfelt thanks,

Justine Ehiwario

DISCLAIMER

The information presented in this book, *The DNA of Financial Greatness*, is intended for educational and informational purposes only. The content reflects the author's personal experiences, beliefs, and research and is not intended to be financial, legal, or investment advice. Readers should consult with a licensed financial advisor, tax professional, or legal counsel before making any financial decisions based on the information provided.

While every effort has been made to ensure the accuracy and completeness of the material, the author and publisher make no guarantees regarding the success or outcomes of any financial actions taken as a result of reading this book. Financial success is influenced by a wide range of factors, including but not limited to individual circumstances, market conditions, and external economic forces. The author and publisher are not responsible for any errors, omissions, or negative outcomes arising from the use of this information.

The strategies, tips, and recommendations presented in this book are based on the author's perspective and are not universally applicable. Success in financial matters requires careful consideration of your personal goals, values, and resources.

By reading this book, you acknowledge that the author, publisher, and any affiliated parties are not liable for any losses or damages, financial or otherwise, incurred as a result of applying the information contained in this book.

Please use the information contained within this book responsibly and exercise due diligence in making any financial decision.

Copyright Notice

© [2025] Justine Ehiwario. All rights reserved.

Preface

Welcome to *The DNA of Financial Greatness*. This book is not just another guide to financial success; it is a blueprint for unlocking your true potential and building a lasting legacy of wealth. Over the years, I've discovered that financial greatness is not an accident—it is a result of intentional decisions, strategic thinking, and the right mindset. My journey toward understanding the intricacies of wealth creation has been filled with lessons, challenges, and breakthroughs, all of which have shaped the principles and strategies shared within these pages.

Financial success is often portrayed as a destination, but in reality, it is a lifelong journey. Along the way, we encounter opportunities, setbacks, and moments of clarity that define our relationship with money and success. What separates those who achieve financial greatness from those who don't is a deep understanding of the principles that govern wealth and the discipline to apply them consistently.

In this book, I've distilled the essential elements of financial mastery into actionable steps. You'll learn not only how to create wealth but also how to sustain and grow it for generations to come. This book is structured to give you practical insights, real-life examples, and a clear path toward building the financial future you deserve.

As you read through these chapters, my hope is that you will gain a deeper understanding of the forces that shape financial success and apply them to your own life. Whether you are just starting your wealth-building journey or looking to refine your existing strategies, this book will provide you with the tools to activate your financial DNA and achieve your goals.

Remember, financial greatness is not defined by the amount of money you accumulate, but by the impact you make and the legacy you leave behind. It's time to activate your potential and step into a future of limitless possibilities.

Thank you for allowing me to be part of your journey toward financial greatness.

Justine Ehiwario
(Engineer, Entrepreneur, Author, and Financial Mentor)

Section 1:

Establishing the Foundation for Financial Achievement (Mindset & Fundamental Principles)

Chapter 1:

Unlocking the Wealth Mindset

The foundation of financial prosperity is deeply rooted in mindset. Our perception of money, wealth, and success has a profound impact on the trajectory of our financial futures. How we think about wealth, opportunities, and the very idea of financial abundance shapes every decision we make, often without our conscious awareness. As I've discussed in my previous works such as *The Unstoppable Road to Wealth Creation*, *The Things Wealthy People Do*, and *The Mind of a Trillionaire*, a person's financial destiny is not determined by external circumstances alone; it is shaped predominantly by the thoughts and beliefs that reside in their minds.

Developing the right mindset is not something that happens overnight. It requires intentional reprogramming, the deliberate effort to replace old, limiting beliefs with new, and empowering ones. The wealthy understand this concept intuitively, and they actively shape their thoughts, attitudes, and habits in ways that foster financial success. They approach money and wealth creation with a mindset of abundance, possibility, and constant growth.

In this chapter, we'll explore how the wealthiest individuals cultivate a mindset that supports their financial goals. We'll uncover the principles and thought patterns that create opportunities, ignite ambition, and pave the way for long-term financial success. Through understanding and applying these principles, you too can develop the mental framework that allows you to unlock your true wealth-building potential.

The Power of Mindset in Wealth Creation

The idea that "mindset is everything" has become a popular mantra in personal development and financial circles, but its truth cannot be overstated. A person's mindset doesn't just affect their mood or emotional state; it directly influences their ability to create wealth. In *The Unstoppable Road to Wealth Creation*, I explain that wealth is not a destination but a journey—and that journey begins in the mind. Financial success is not just about having access to resources or opportunities; it's about how we perceive and respond to those resources.

Wealthy individuals see opportunities where others see obstacles. They approach challenges with optimism and resilience, knowing that every difficulty is an opportunity for growth. This mindset is not accidental. It is cultivated through continuous personal development and the deliberate reprogramming of old thought patterns.

Illustrative Example:

Consider two individuals who both face financial setbacks. One of them views the situation as a failure, feels defeated, and ultimately gives up on their financial goals. The other sees the setback as a temporary hurdle, analyzes the lessons to be learned from it, and uses the experience to improve their approach moving forward. The second individual's mindset aligns with the principles I discuss in *The Things Wealthy People Do*, where I highlight that the wealthy view adversity as a stepping stone toward success.

What separates these two individuals is the way they approach challenges—one with a mindset of scarcity and defeat, the other with a mindset of abundance and growth. The wealthy do not allow temporary setbacks to define their financial future; instead, they take each challenge as an opportunity to learn and grow, ultimately accelerating their journey toward wealth.

The Role of Beliefs in Shaping Financial Success

In *The Mind of a Trillionaire*, I delve into how beliefs about money and success are the building blocks of wealth. These beliefs shape our financial behavior, influencing how we manage money, make investments, and approach opportunities. The most common limiting beliefs are those that suggest that wealth is out of reach or that money is inherently difficult to acquire. These beliefs, often inherited from our families or influenced by societal norms, create subconscious barriers that prevent us from achieving financial success.

Common Limiting Beliefs About Money:

1. "Money doesn't grow on trees."

2. "You have to work extremely hard to get rich."

3. "Rich people are selfish or unethical."

4. "I'm just not good with money."

These beliefs are often deeply ingrained and can create a subconscious resistance to wealth-building activities. If you've ever caught yourself thinking that "rich people are lucky" or "I'll never be able to afford that," you're engaging with one of these limiting beliefs. The truth, however, is that wealth is a skill—a mindset that can be developed, honed, and mastered with the right approach.

In contrast, wealthy individuals hold empowering beliefs about money. They believe that wealth is a tool that can be used to create value, solve problems, and achieve greater goals. They understand that money is not the goal itself but a means to live a fulfilling and impactful life. This mindset allows them to seek out opportunities that others might miss, and it fuels their relentless drive toward financial independence and success.

Illustrative Example:

Take the case of an entrepreneur who has a belief that "money is a tool to solve problems." This person might start a business that addresses a specific market need, using their profits to reinvest into new ventures or philanthropic endeavors. They do not view money as the end goal, but as the means to create value and make a positive impact in their community.

On the other hand, someone who believes "money is the root of all evil" might hesitate to take the necessary steps to earn and grow wealth, viewing financial success as something morally wrong. These beliefs will likely limit their actions, keeping them trapped in a cycle of financial struggle.

Abundance vs. Scarcity Mindset

One of the most crucial elements of a wealth-oriented mindset is the concept of abundance versus scarcity. In *The Unstoppable Road to Wealth Creation*, I discuss how individuals with an abundance mindset see the world as full of opportunities. They believe that there is enough wealth, success, and resources to go around. This mindset drives them to take calculated risks, invest in opportunities, and pursue their goals with confidence.

On the other hand, individuals with a scarcity mindset see the world as competitive and limited. They believe that resources are scarce and that if one person succeeds, it must come at the expense of others. This belief causes them to hold onto what they have out of fear of losing it, making them risk-averse and reluctant to invest in their future.

Illustrative Example:

Consider the difference between two investors. One has an abundance mindset and is willing to diversify their portfolio, invest in real estate, stocks, and other assets. They understand that wealth is not a zero-sum game—if someone else succeeds, it doesn't mean they will fail. The other investor, with a scarcity mindset, is afraid to take any risks and only keeps their money in a savings account, fearing that any investment could result in loss.

The first investor, embracing the abundance mindset, is likely to see better returns in the long run, as they are open to new opportunities and are willing to take calculated risks. The second investor, held back by fear and limited beliefs, may see little to no growth in their wealth.

The Wealthy Mindset: Thinking Like a Trillionaire

In *The Mind of a Trillionaire*, I explore how the world's wealthiest individuals—those who have accumulated vast fortunes—think about money and wealth creation. These individuals have learned to think strategically, approach opportunities with creativity, and view failure as part of the learning process. They are not deterred by obstacles or setbacks; instead, they see each challenge as a chance to improve.

Trillionaires and billionaires think differently from the average person. They don't simply work to survive—they work to innovate, create, and disrupt. They are forward-thinking and invest in the future, understanding that wealth is not just about accumulating money but about shaping industries and impacting society on a global scale.

Illustrative Example:

Take Jeff Bezos, founder of Amazon. Bezos didn't start Amazon with the goal of simply making money. He started Amazon because he saw an opportunity to revolutionize how people shop and access goods. His mindset was focused on long-term success, innovation, and making a profound impact on the world. As a result, Amazon has grown into one of the largest and most influential companies in the world.

Bezos' mindset is one of the core principles that I discuss in *The Mind of a Trillionaire*. His ability to think beyond immediate profits and focus on long-term growth is a hallmark of the wealth mindset.

Shifting Your Mindset for Financial Success

Changing your mindset is not a one-time event; it's an ongoing process. It requires consistency, patience, and a willingness to let go of outdated beliefs. In *The Things Wealthy People Do*, I highlight the importance of daily habits in shaping the mind of a successful individual. Successful people don't just think differently; they live differently. They consistently engage in practices that reinforce their wealth-building mindset.

To shift your mindset, start by practicing the following steps:

1. **Surround Yourself with Positive Influences:** The people you associate with have a significant impact on your mindset. Surround yourself with individuals who have an abundance mindset, who encourage your growth, and who challenge you to think bigger. In *The Unstoppable Road to Wealth Creation*, I

explain how the right network can accelerate your financial journey.

2. **Reframe Limiting Beliefs:** Every time you catch yourself thinking negatively about money, reframe it. Replace thoughts like "I'll never be able to afford this" with "I am capable of finding ways to make this happen." Over time, this will shift your perception and open you up to new opportunities.

3. **Take Inspired Action:** A mindset shift is only effective if it's paired with action. In *The Things Wealthy People Do*, I discuss how successful individuals don't just think about success—they act on their thoughts. Whether it's starting a new business, making an investment, or learning a new skill, taking action is key to manifesting your wealth.

Conclusion: The Power of a Wealth-Oriented Mindset

Unlocking the wealth mindset is the first and most crucial step toward financial success. As we've discussed in this chapter, the way you think about money and wealth directly impacts your financial future. By understanding and adopting the principles that drive the wealthiest individuals, you can begin to shift your mindset and take intentional action toward building lasting wealth.

In *The Unstoppable Road to Wealth Creation*, *The Things Wealthy People Do*, and *The Mind of a Trillionaire*, I have shared practical strategies for cultivating a wealth-oriented mindset. It's time for you to unlock your own potential by changing the way you think, speak, and act around money. As you do, you'll find that opportunities begin to present themselves in abundance, and your financial future will be shaped by your thoughts, beliefs, and actions.

34

Chapter 2:

Overcoming Financial Roadblocks

Financial growth isn't merely hindered by external factors such as lack of resources, opportunities, or favorable market conditions. Often, the most significant barriers to wealth creation are the mental roadblocks we place around money. These mental obstacles are deeply embedded in our subconscious and are formed through experiences, beliefs, and societal conditioning. In *The Unstoppable Road to Wealth Creation*, *The Things Wealthy People Do*, and *The Mind of a Trillionaire*, I discuss the role of mindset in financial success, underscoring how mental barriers—often built without conscious awareness—prevent many from reaching their full financial potential.

In this chapter, we will explore the most common financial roadblocks, how they manifest, and how you can dismantle them. These roadblocks are often based on limiting beliefs and attitudes formed in childhood or reinforced by societal norms. Phrases such as "money doesn't grow on trees," "only the lucky get rich," or "wealth is for the few" are ingrained in many people's minds and influence their decisions, often without them realizing it. Understanding how to identify and overcome these limiting beliefs is the key to breaking free from financial stagnation and stepping into a life of financial success.

The Foundation of Financial Roadblocks: The Influence of Beliefs

To understand how roadblocks form, we first need to look at how beliefs are shaped. Our beliefs about money are formed in our early years, often by the people we are closest to—our parents, guardians, teachers, and community. A child raised in an environment where money is scarce will likely internalize a scarcity mindset, believing that money is difficult to come by. Similarly, if they are raised hearing that wealth is only for the "lucky" or "privileged," they may grow up believing that financial success is out of their control.

In *The Unstoppable Road to Wealth Creation*, I discuss how these beliefs can be deeply ingrained in our subconscious, affecting our behavior without us even realizing it. These subconscious beliefs create mental blocks that keep us from taking the necessary steps to build wealth. The road to financial success begins with recognizing these blocks and deciding to dismantle them.

Identifying the Common Financial Roadblocks

While everyone's financial journey is unique, there are several common mental barriers that prevent people from achieving financial success. Below are some of the most common roadblocks and how they manifest in daily life.

1. The Scarcity Mindset

A scarcity mindset is perhaps the most pervasive mental roadblock to financial success. People with a scarcity mindset view money as limited, as though there's never enough to go around. They often feel that any success achieved by others diminishes their own chances of success. This mindset is rooted in fear—the fear of not having enough and the fear of losing what little they have.

In *The Things Wealthy People Do*, I emphasize how the wealthy, in contrast, adopt an abundance mindset. Instead of seeing money as finite, they see it as a tool that is constantly replenished as long as it is put to work. Scarcity thinking keeps people stuck in a cycle of fear and self-doubt, which ultimately leads to inaction.

Illustrative Example:

Take the case of a person who grew up in a household where money was always tight. As an adult, they might hold onto every penny, fearing that spending any money will result in them not having enough. This person might resist investing or taking calculated risks, even when they have opportunities to grow their wealth. The fear of scarcity causes them to miss out on opportunities for financial growth, perpetuating the cycle of financial stagnation.

Solution:

Shifting from a scarcity mindset to an abundance mindset is one of the most powerful steps in overcoming financial roadblocks. To do this, start by acknowledging and being grateful for what you have, no matter how small it may seem. As I discussed in *The Unstoppable Road to Wealth Creation*, a mindset shift requires actively seeking opportunities to grow, rather than fearing loss. Wealth is a mindset—if you believe there's always enough, you'll begin to see new ways to create and multiply your financial resources.

2. The Fear of Failure

The fear of failure is another significant roadblock in wealth creation. Many people are afraid to take risks or try new ventures because they fear failing. This fear is often rooted in past experiences of failure, societal pressure to succeed, or negative reinforcement from others. As a result, people with a fear of failure may avoid taking the actions necessary to create wealth, staying in their comfort zones and sticking to what's safe and familiar.

In *The Mind of a Trillionaire*, I explore how the most successful individuals view failure as an inevitable and valuable part of the success process. Instead of seeing failure as a sign of incompetence, wealthy individuals see it as a necessary part of learning and growth. Failure is a teacher, not a punishment.

Illustrative Example:

Consider someone who wants to start a business but is terrified of failing. They may never take the first step in launching their venture, despite having a solid business idea. This fear of failure keeps them stuck in a job they don't enjoy, wondering "what if" they could have succeeded if they had just tried. Unfortunately, by not taking action, they are unknowingly ensuring their financial stagnation.

Solution:

Overcoming the fear of failure requires a shift in perspective. In *The Things Wealthy People Do*, I discuss how successful individuals take calculated risks, fail, and learn from their mistakes. Instead of allowing failure to discourage them, they view it as a stepping stone toward success. To overcome this roadblock, focus on taking small, actionable steps toward your goals. Celebrate each failure as a learning experience and use it to adjust your approach.

3. Limiting Beliefs About Money

Limiting beliefs about money are deeply ingrained in many individuals. These beliefs stem from past experiences, societal conditioning, or cultural influences and can include thoughts such as "I'm not good with money," "Only the rich can afford to invest," or "I'll never be able to make that much money." These beliefs limit one's ability to act in a way that fosters wealth creation.

In *The Unstoppable Road to Wealth Creation*, I explore how these limiting beliefs can shape a person's financial future. They become self-fulfilling prophecies, with individuals subconsciously sabotaging their own success because they believe they are unworthy or incapable of creating wealth. To break free from these limiting beliefs, one must first recognize them and replace them with empowering beliefs.

Illustrative Example:

A person might believe they are "bad with money" because of past financial mistakes. This belief might prevent them from managing their finances properly, leading to more mistakes and reinforcing the idea that they can never be good with money. Over time, this belief becomes a barrier to financial growth.

Solution:

To overcome limiting beliefs about money, start by acknowledging and challenging them. Ask yourself: "Why do I believe this? Is it true? How has this belief served me?" Reframe your thoughts by replacing limiting beliefs with empowering ones. For example, instead of thinking "I'm bad with money," change it to "I am learning how to manage my money better each day." In *The Things Wealthy People Do*, I explain how wealthy individuals cultivate a mindset that aligns with abundance, and how you can do the same.

4. Lack of Financial Education

One of the most common financial roadblocks is a lack of financial literacy.

Without understanding the basics of budgeting, saving, investing, and growing wealth, it's easy to make poor financial decisions. Financial illiteracy often results from a lack of formal education on the subject, and without the proper knowledge, it becomes challenging to build wealth.

In *The Unstoppable Road to Wealth Creation*, I stress the importance of continuous financial education. Wealthy individuals make it a point to stay informed about financial trends, investment strategies, and wealth-building opportunities. They know that knowledge is power, and the more they learn, the better equipped they are to make informed decisions that will benefit their financial future.

Illustrative Example:

A person might have a steady job and earn a decent income but fail to take advantage of opportunities to invest or grow their wealth. They might not know where to start or what options are available to them. Without the proper financial education, they miss opportunities that could lead to significant wealth.

Solution:

The key to overcoming financial illiteracy is education. Take the time to learn about budgeting, saving, investing, and growing wealth. In *The Mind of a Trillionaire*, I provide practical advice on how to educate yourself and build a solid financial foundation. Whether through books, online courses, or mentorship, gaining financial knowledge is essential for breaking free from this roadblock.

Taking Action: Shifting from Knowledge to Execution

It's one thing to understand the roadblocks to financial success, but it's another to take action and break free from them. Overcoming financial roadblocks requires a mindset shift coupled with consistent, intentional action. As I discussed in *The Unstoppable Road to Wealth Creation*, taking consistent action—no matter how small—can help you break free from mental constraints and start building the wealth you desire.

Illustrative Example:

Imagine someone who, after years of being held back by mental roadblocks, finally decides to take action. They start by setting a budget, investing a small amount in the stock market, and educating themselves on financial matters. Over time, their confidence grows, and they begin to see results, which further fuels their desire to continue building their wealth.

Solution:

Taking action means setting clear financial goals, developing a plan to achieve them, and executing that plan consistently. The most successful people are those who don't just think about their goals—they act on them. In *The Mind of a Trillionaire*, I emphasize the importance of turning ideas into action and how wealth is built not just by thinking big, but by acting boldly.

Conclusion: Transforming Your Financial Destiny

Overcoming financial roadblocks is a crucial step toward building lasting wealth. It requires awareness, persistence, and a commitment to changing the way you think about money. By addressing and dismantling the limiting beliefs, fears, and misconceptions that hold you back, you create the mental space necessary for financial growth. And when you combine this mindset shift with practical action, you set yourself on a path toward financial freedom and prosperity.

In *The Unstoppable Road to Wealth Creation*, *The Things Wealthy People Do*, and *The Mind of a Trillionaire*, I have shared strategies that can help you break through these roadblocks and take control of your financial future. The road to wealth is not easy, but with the right mindset and the willingness to take action, it is more than achievable.

Chapter 3:

The DNA of Financial Success

Just like every individual has a unique genetic makeup, each person's financial success is influenced by their habits and routines. Our daily actions, decisions, and the routines we engage in determine the financial outcomes we experience. Financial success is not solely about big, dramatic actions—it is the sum of countless small, consistent decisions that align with wealth-building principles.

As I've explored in *The Unstoppable Road to Wealth Creation*, *The Things Wealthy People Do*, and *The Mind of a Trillionaire*, these everyday habits and routines are the DNA of financial success. They form the foundation for long-term growth and prosperity, making them an essential element of any wealth-building strategy. In this chapter, we will dive into these small yet powerful habits—such as saving a percentage of income, making strategic financial decisions, and investing in self-education—and explore how they can be transformed into a framework for financial achievement.

The goal of this chapter is to show that financial success is not reserved for a select few. Anyone, regardless of their background or circumstances, can begin to cultivate habits that lead to financial independence. The secret lies in the ability to understand how habits shape our financial futures and, most importantly, how we can modify our routines to align with our financial goals.

Understanding the DNA of Financial Success

When we think about wealth, it's easy to focus on the large, obvious milestones: a big business deal, a successful investment, or a major career breakthrough. However, true and lasting financial success is not just built on these "big wins." In fact, it is often the result of small, consistent actions that accumulate over time. Just like the biological DNA of an individual determines their traits and characteristics, your financial "DNA" is defined by the daily choices and habits you consistently make.

In *The Unstoppable Road to Wealth Creation*, I emphasize that building wealth is a process that requires consistent action over time. It's the daily commitment to your financial goals, the discipline to follow through on smart money management habits, and the willingness to continuously learn and improve that shapes your financial trajectory.

The Power of Small Habits: Why Consistency Wins

Many people believe that achieving financial success requires a sudden breakthrough, an overnight success, or a massive windfall. In *The Things*

Wealthy People Do, I argue that true financial growth comes not from luck, but from mastering small, consistent habits over time. The wealthy understand this principle: financial success is not an event, but a journey made up of small, disciplined steps.

Illustrative Example:

Imagine two individuals starting from scratch, both of whom want to build wealth. One individual starts investing $100 per month, while the other waits for the "right opportunity" to invest. Ten years later, the individual who made consistent monthly contributions has accumulated wealth through compound interest, while the other person, despite having the same amount of money to invest, has nothing to show for it because they waited for the "perfect time." The key difference? The first person understood that small, consistent actions add up over time.

Habit #1: Saving and Budgeting

One of the most foundational habits in the DNA of financial success is saving and budgeting. A large part of wealth creation involves making sure you live within your means and consistently set aside a percentage of your income for future investments. While budgeting is often seen as a restrictive practice, in *The Mind of a Trillionaire*, I discuss how the wealthy view budgeting not as a limitation, but as a powerful tool for financial freedom. By allocating a set portion of your income for savings and investments, you are ensuring that your money works for you, even when you're not actively working for it.

The importance of saving cannot be overstated. Financial experts recommend saving at least 10-20% of your income, depending on your financial goals. However, it's not just about setting aside money—it's about creating a habit of saving. The wealthy are disciplined in their approach to saving, ensuring that every paycheck contributes to their long-term wealth-building strategy.

Illustrative Example:

Consider the case of an individual who consistently saves 15% of their monthly income. Over time, they accumulate a substantial amount of capital, which they can then use to make strategic investments. In contrast, someone who spends every penny of their income without a savings plan may never experience financial growth, regardless of their income level. The key difference lies in the habit of saving—this is the cornerstone of financial success.

Habit #2: Investing in Self-Education

In *The Unstoppable Road to Wealth Creation*, I emphasize the importance of investing in yourself. One of the habits that separates the wealthy from the average person is their relentless pursuit of knowledge and self-improvement. The wealthy understand that financial success is not just about earning money, but about continually improving their skills, knowledge, and understanding of money management.

The richest individuals dedicate a significant portion of their time and resources to acquiring new knowledge, whether it's through reading, attending seminars, or learning from mentors. In *The Things Wealthy People Do*, I explore how wealthy individuals commit to lifelong learning as a key driver of their financial success. They understand that knowledge empowers them to make smarter decisions, spot opportunities, and adapt to an ever-changing financial landscape.

Illustrative Example:

Consider Warren Buffet, one of the wealthiest individuals in the world. Buffet spends a large portion of his day reading and learning about different industries, companies, and economic trends. This commitment to self-education has allowed him to make wise investment decisions that have accumulated over decades. As I mention in *The Mind of a Trillionaire*, Buffet's success can be attributed not only to his financial acumen but also to his commitment to lifelong learning.

Habit #3: Making Smart Financial Decisions

Making smart financial decisions is an essential habit that forms part of the DNA of financial success. Every decision—whether it's choosing to buy a home, taking on debt, or investing in a business—affects your financial future. The wealthy understand that every dollar spent or invested has the potential to either move them closer to or further from their financial goals.

In *The Mind of a Trillionaire*, I dive deep into how billionaires and Trillionaires make calculated decisions about where to allocate their resources. They are meticulous in their financial planning, often considering the long-term implications of their choices. For instance, they understand the power of compound interest and leverage, using both to build wealth over time.

Smart financial decisions also involve knowing when to take risks and when to be conservative. The wealthy are not afraid of taking risks, but they understand the importance of managing and mitigating those risks through research, planning, and expert advice.

Illustrative Example:

Look at the decision-making process of someone like Elon Musk, whose ventures—such as Tesla and SpaceX—are built on calculated risks. Musk has made bold decisions that have paid off, but these decisions are always backed by thorough research and an understanding of potential rewards and risks. In contrast, someone who consistently makes poor financial decisions without a strategy or understanding of risk is likely to encounter setbacks that prevent financial growth.

Habit #4: Building Multiple Streams of Income

In *The Unstoppable Road to Wealth Creation*, I explain that building multiple streams of income is crucial for long-term financial growth. Relying solely on one source of income—whether it's a salary or business—leaves you vulnerable to unexpected changes in your financial situation. The wealthy, however, diversify their income streams, creating multiple avenues for earning money and building wealth.

These income streams can include investments, real estate, royalties, business ventures, or even side hustles. The key is to build systems that generate income independently of your daily active work. The more diverse your income sources, the less dependent you are on any single source, giving you greater financial security.

Illustrative Example:

Consider someone who has income from multiple sources: a regular job, a rental property, an online business, and stock investments. If one income source is temporarily interrupted, they have others to rely on. This diversification ensures that they can weather financial storms without significant disruption to their wealth-building plan.

Habit #5: Long-Term Thinking

One of the most defining characteristics of wealthy individuals is their ability to think long-term. In *The Mind of a Trillionaire*, I discuss how billionaires often make decisions based on long-term goals rather than short-term gratification. This long-term thinking is evident in their investment strategies, business planning, and personal wealth management.

Wealthy individuals don't chase quick profits or instant gratification. They understand that true wealth is built over time through disciplined investments, strategic decisions, and careful planning. They are willing to delay immediate rewards in favor of greater, long-term financial success.

Illustrative Example:

Jeff Bezos, the founder of Amazon, famously reinvested nearly all of Amazon's profits back into the business during its early years. He prioritized long-term growth over short-term profits, a decision that ultimately made him one of the wealthiest individuals in the world. This long-term thinking is a key element of his financial success, as discussed in

The Things Wealthy People Do.

Conclusion: The DNA of Financial Success

The small habits and daily routines we adopt form the core of our financial success. In this chapter, we've explored the habits that make up the DNA of financial success: saving and budgeting, investing in self-education, making smart financial decisions, building multiple income streams, and adopting a long-term perspective.

As we've seen, financial success is not about having the most money upfront or making a single big decision. It's about consistently making smart choices that align with your long-term financial goals. By adopting these habits and incorporating them into your daily routines, you'll lay the foundation for lasting financial prosperity.

In *The Unstoppable Road to Wealth Creation*, *The Things Wealthy People Do*, and *The Mind of a Trillionaire*, I've shared how these habits are vital for achieving financial freedom. By building them into your life, you'll begin to see your financial trajectory shift toward growth, stability, and success. The DNA of financial success is within your grasp—it's up to you to activate it.

Chapter 4:

Mastering Wealth Acceleration

In the pursuit of financial prosperity, the journey from modest beginnings to wealth can seem like a slow and arduous process. However, there are proven strategies that can significantly accelerate this journey, pushing you closer to your financial goals much faster than conventional methods. Wealth doesn't grow overnight, but there are ways to compress the timeline by leveraging high-return investments, identifying lucrative opportunities, and making bold yet calculated moves. This chapter is about mastering the strategies that can exponentially multiply your financial resources—smart risk-taking, generating passive income, and capitalizing on high-leverage ventures.

As explored in *The Unstoppable Road to Wealth Creation*, *The Things Wealthy People Do*, and *The Mind of a Trillionaire*, accelerating wealth accumulation is a key element of financial success. It's not about just making more money; it's about multiplying your money and putting it to work for you. To truly accelerate wealth, you must understand the mechanics behind investments, the power of leverage, and how to capitalize on the opportunities that present themselves in the marketplace. Let's explore these techniques and strategies in depth.

The Power of High-Return Investments

The most efficient way to accelerate wealth is by making your money work for you. High-return investments—such as stocks, real estate, businesses, or even alternative investments—are key drivers of wealth acceleration. While not without risk, these types of investments offer the potential for significant returns, often far outpacing traditional savings accounts or low-risk investments.

The Role of Stock Market Investments:

In *The Unstoppable Road to Wealth Creation*, I emphasize the importance of smart, long-term stock market investments as a vehicle for wealth growth. The stock market provides the potential for compounding returns, particularly through dividend reinvestment and capital gains. While the market can be volatile in the short term, over the long run, it has proven to be one of the most reliable ways to accumulate wealth.

For instance, consider the case of someone who consistently invests in index funds or blue-chip stocks, companies that have historically delivered stable returns. While the growth may seem slow at first, the power of compounding accelerates over time, allowing that individual to build a significant wealth base. The key here is patience and strategic investment in the right assets.

Illustrative Example:

In *The Things Wealthy People Do*, I discuss the power of Warren Buffett's investment strategy. Buffet has long been a proponent of value investing—finding stocks that are undervalued and holding them for the long term. By doing this, he's been able to build an enormous fortune, using the principle of buying good companies at a low price and holding them until their value grows. The lesson here is that strategic, high-return investments, when chosen wisely, provide a solid foundation for accelerating wealth.

Leveraging Real Estate for Wealth Growth

Real estate is another critical vehicle for wealth acceleration. Real estate provides both immediate cash flow through rental income and long-term wealth appreciation. Property investments can also be highly leveraged, meaning you can use a small amount of your own money (a down payment) to control a much larger asset, which is a powerful way to accelerate the growth of your wealth.

In *The Unstoppable Road to Wealth Creation*, I detail how the wealthy often use real estate as a cornerstone of their financial portfolios. Not only does real estate provide a tangible asset that appreciates over time, but it also offers passive income opportunities through rental properties. Moreover, real estate can provide tax advantages and serve as a hedge against inflation, further boosting its appeal as an investment class.

Illustrative Example:

Imagine an individual who purchases rental properties with a small down payment but rents them out for consistent monthly cash flow. Over time, as the properties appreciate in value, the wealth accumulated from these properties grows exponentially. By leveraging financing options such as mortgages, the individual can acquire multiple properties, multiplying the returns significantly. This is a practical example of wealth acceleration—using leverage to scale investments.

Passive Income: Making Money While You Sleep

The ultimate goal of wealth accumulation is financial freedom—the ability to make money without constantly working for it. Passive income is the golden ticket to achieving this goal. Passive income can come from various sources, such as rental income, dividends, royalties, affiliate marketing, and digital products.

In *The Mind of a Trillionaire*, I discuss how the wealthiest individuals actively seek out opportunities to generate passive income streams. The ability to earn without direct effort is a key to accelerating wealth, as it allows money to flow in continuously without requiring constant input.

Illustrative Example:

Consider the case of someone who writes a book or creates an online course. Once the initial work is done, the book or course continues to generate revenue with little to no ongoing effort. The more passive income streams you can create, the faster your wealth will grow, as each one contributes to the larger goal of financial independence.

The Power of Smart Risk-Taking

Risk is an inevitable part of wealth acceleration. The wealthiest individuals understand the importance of taking calculated risks. In *The Unstoppable Road to Wealth Creation*, I stress that risk is a key component of financial growth, but it must be managed carefully. Wealthy individuals take risks that have the potential for significant rewards, but they do so with careful research, strategic planning, and an understanding of the odds.

Smart risk-taking isn't about gambling—it's about making informed decisions that have the potential to yield high rewards. For instance, an entrepreneur starting a business may take on debt to finance their venture, but they do so because they believe that the return on investment (ROI) will far exceed the risk involved.

In *The Things Wealthy People Do*, I detail how billionaires like Elon Musk and Richard Branson have built their fortunes by embracing risk in industries that were considered high-risk but high-reward. Both have been willing to take on large amounts of personal and financial risk, but their investments have often paid off handsomely due to the high leverage and potential return in the industries they've chosen.

Identifying and Capitalizing on Opportunities

Wealth acceleration requires an acute ability to identify opportunities when they arise. In *The Mind of a Trillionaire*, I explore how billionaires and high-net-worth individuals have an uncanny ability to spot opportunities that others may overlook. These opportunities could be in the form of emerging markets, new technologies, or unique investment opportunities.

An individual's ability to recognize and capitalize on these opportunities is a key differentiator between those who build wealth quickly and those who don't. Wealthy individuals often have a well-developed network, a keen sense of market trends, and an ability to take action when the time is right.

Illustrative Example:

Look at the rise of tech companies like Google and Facebook. In their early days, the founders recognized the untapped potential of the internet and acted quickly to capitalize on it. By positioning themselves early in a growing industry, they accelerated their wealth accumulation at a rate that traditional industries simply couldn't match.

High-Leverage Ventures and Building Wealth Through Business

One of the most powerful ways to accelerate wealth is by building and scaling a business. Owning a business allows you to control your financial destiny, and with the right business model, it's possible to see rapid growth in a relatively short period of time.

In *The Unstoppable Road to Wealth Creation*, I emphasize that business ownership is a critical path to wealth acceleration. Whether you're starting a small side hustle or building a large-scale enterprise, the principles of business growth—leveraging people, resources, and capital—can drastically speed up your wealth-building journey.

Illustrative Example:

Consider Jeff Bezos and the early days of Amazon. Bezos started with a small online bookstore and leveraged the power of the internet to scale rapidly. By reinvesting the profits and focusing on growth over short-term profits, he created a global empire that transformed the retail industry and accelerated his wealth at an unprecedented rate.

Strategic Debt and Leverage

Another component of wealth acceleration is the smart use of debt. While debt can be a tool for financial distress if misused, wealthy individuals understand how to use debt strategically to scale their investments. Leverage allows you to control larger assets and investments with a smaller amount of your own capital.

In *The Mind of a Trillionaire*, I discuss how the wealthy use leverage in the form of mortgages, business loans, and even private equity to scale their wealth rapidly. Strategic debt, when used correctly, can amplify returns on investments and create the foundation for exponential growth.

Conclusion: Accelerating Your Wealth Journey

Wealth acceleration is not about making one big gamble or hoping for a stroke of luck. It's about adopting smart, strategic practices that put your money to work for you. From high-return investments to leveraging passive income, smart risk-taking, and scaling businesses, there are multiple strategies you can employ to accelerate your wealth accumulation.

As discussed in *The Unstoppable Road to Wealth Creation*, *The Things Wealthy People Do*, and *The Mind of a Trillionaire*, the wealthy are intentional about how they build their wealth, leveraging opportunities and managing risk along the way. By adopting these strategies, you too can begin to accelerate your financial growth and move closer to the financial freedom you desire.

Remember, wealth acceleration requires patience, persistence, and a commitment to continuous improvement. Implementing these strategies and honing your ability to spot opportunities, take risks, and leverage your resources will not only accelerate your wealth journey but will also set you on the path to long-term financial success.

Chapter 5:

Financial Knowledge as a Power Tool

"Knowledge is power." This timeless adage is especially relevant in the realm of finance. The truth is, acquiring and mastering financial knowledge provides a critical edge that can separate the wealthy from the average. While many people might think that financial success is simply about having more money, the truth is that the ability to manage, grow, and protect wealth stems directly from one's understanding of financial concepts.

In *The Unstoppable Road to Wealth Creation*, *The Things Wealthy People Do*, and *The Mind of a Trillionaire*, I explore how financial literacy isn't just a supplementary skill; it is the very foundation of wealth accumulation and long-term financial success. Understanding the key elements of finance—from investing to tax strategies to personal finance—is not just beneficial; it is essential for anyone aiming to achieve significant wealth. This chapter will delve into the importance of financial knowledge and how the richest individuals continuously educate themselves, often learning from others' mistakes, staying ahead of trends, and using financial knowledge to their advantage.

Why Financial Knowledge Matters

Most wealthy individuals did not achieve their status overnight. Rather, they spent years learning, experimenting, and adapting to the complexities of money management. Financial knowledge allows individuals to make informed decisions that maximize wealth-building opportunities while minimizing the risks involved.

Financial knowledge can be broken down into a few essential components:

1. **Investing** – Understanding how to put your money to work is a skill that separates the average from the extraordinary.

2. **Tax Strategies** – Knowing how to minimize taxes and take advantage of tax incentives can dramatically impact wealth accumulation.

3. **Personal Finance** – Managing your daily finances, budgeting effectively, saving, and planning for the future are all foundational elements of financial mastery.

By mastering these concepts, wealthy individuals gain an invaluable tool to amplify their wealth, while the average person often remains stuck in financial stagnation. In this chapter, we'll explore the key areas of financial knowledge and how they directly correlate with wealth-building.

Investing: Making Your Money Work for You

Investing is one of the most critical elements of wealth-building. Understanding how to grow your money through investments is not just a luxury for the rich; it's a necessity. In *The Unstoppable Road to Wealth Creation*, I emphasize the power of strategic investments. Whether it's stocks, real estate, or other assets, investing allows money to grow beyond the pace of inflation and creates compounding wealth over time.

Illustrative Example:

Take, for instance, the story of Warren Buffett, one of the wealthiest individuals in the world. In *The Mind of a Trillionaire*, I discuss how Buffett's understanding of investing has been the driving force behind his incredible success. He doesn't simply buy companies for the sake of investing; he looks for companies with strong fundamentals, good management, and a sustainable business model. His investment strategy is rooted in sound knowledge of finance and business operations.

Buffett's story underscores a central theme that I discuss in *The Things Wealthy People Do*: financial success isn't a matter of luck; it's about applying financial knowledge with patience and consistency. The wealthiest people don't just invest to make quick gains; they invest with the intention of creating long-term value. This focus on sustainable growth allows them to build a robust financial portfolio that steadily multiplies over time.

Tax Strategies: Protecting Wealth from Unnecessary Losses

A critical aspect of financial knowledge that is often overlooked is understanding tax strategies. Taxes are a significant burden on personal and business finances. Wealthy individuals, however, understand how to minimize their tax liabilities, using legal strategies such as tax-deferred investments, tax credits, and deductions to keep more of their money.

In *The Unstoppable Road to Wealth Creation*, I detail how tax strategies play a pivotal role in wealth preservation. Rich individuals often consult with tax experts and financial advisors who help them optimize their tax position, allowing them to invest and grow their wealth without facing excessive tax burdens.

Illustrative Example:

Consider the example of real estate investors. In *The Mind of a Trillionaire*, I discuss how real estate investors use tax strategies to their advantage. For instance, real estate investors can take advantage of tax-deferred strategies such as 1031 exchanges, which allow them to defer paying taxes on profits from a sale as long as they reinvest the proceeds into another property. This strategy allows them to build wealth without being immediately taxed on their profits, allowing for greater reinvestment and growth.

In *The Things Wealthy People Do*, I also highlight how individuals who are not financially literate may miss out on these kinds of opportunities. For the average person, taxes might seem like a fixed burden, but for the financially knowledgeable, they are merely an obstacle to navigate. Mastering tax strategies can save individuals hundreds of thousands, if not millions, of dollars over their lifetimes.

Personal Finance: The Foundation of Wealth Building

The foundation of wealth-building starts with personal finance. Understanding how to manage your money—creating budgets, saving, and planning for the future—is fundamental to achieving financial success. Without sound personal finance practices, even the most lucrative investments or business ventures can falter.

In *The Unstoppable Road to Wealth Creation*, I explore how successful individuals start by managing their income and expenditures wisely. The first step toward creating wealth is ensuring that you are living below your means, saving, and investing a portion of your income. The richest individuals understand the power of delayed gratification and are disciplined in their financial habits. They also prioritize building an emergency fund, paying off high-interest debt, and making prudent decisions with their resources.

Illustrative Example:

Look at how the wealthy manage their spending. Unlike the average person, they do not succumb to lifestyle inflation—the tendency to increase spending as income increases. Instead, they maintain a frugal lifestyle while allocating a large portion of their earnings into investments and business ventures. For example, in *The Things Wealthy People Do*, I highlight how individuals like Elon Musk and Jeff Bezos have carefully managed their finances, living relatively modest lives despite their billions, and channeling their wealth into ventures that build more wealth.

Financial Education: The Ongoing Process

In addition to understanding specific financial concepts, wealthy individuals often make financial education an ongoing pursuit. They read books, attend seminars, and seek mentorship from those who have already achieved the level of success they aspire to.

In *The Mind of a Trillionaire*, I explore how the most successful people in the world are relentless in their pursuit of knowledge. They see financial education as a lifelong commitment, and they constantly seek new ways to expand their financial understanding. This continuous learning ensures that they stay ahead of financial trends and market shifts, enabling them to make informed decisions that drive wealth accumulation.

Illustrative Example:

Many self-made billionaires have emphasized the importance of lifelong learning. Bill Gates, for instance, famously reads at least one book a week, often focusing on subjects outside of technology and business to expand his understanding of the world. This mindset of constantly seeking new knowledge is a cornerstone of financial success.

In *The Things Wealthy People Do*, I discuss how acquiring financial knowledge is an ongoing process that doesn't end with a single book or seminar. It's about continuously applying new ideas, learning from failures, and evolving with the times.

Mentorship: Learning from the Experiences of Others

While self-education is crucial, mentorship accelerates learning in ways that personal study alone cannot. In *The Unstoppable Road to Wealth Creation*, I emphasize the value of seeking mentorship from those who have already walked the path of financial success. Mentors provide valuable insights, guide you through challenges, and hold you accountable to your goals.

Wealthy individuals often surround themselves with knowledgeable mentors, whether through formal relationships or informal networks. This allows them to gain access to decades of experience and expertise, helping them avoid common pitfalls and stay on the path to financial prosperity.

Illustrative Example:

One famous example is that of Steve Jobs and his mentorship under Robert Noyce, co-founder of Intel. Jobs learned valuable lessons about technology, business, and leadership that helped him shape Apple into the global powerhouse it is today. By seeking guidance from those who have achieved success, individuals can shorten their learning curve and avoid making costly mistakes.

Conclusion: Empowering Your Financial Journey Through Knowledge

Mastering financial knowledge is not optional for those who wish to achieve significant wealth—it is a requirement. The wealthiest individuals in the world understand that knowledge is the key to making smart financial decisions, minimizing risks, and capitalizing on opportunities. By constantly educating themselves, seeking mentorship, and applying the principles of investing, tax strategies, and personal finance, they gain a competitive edge that allows them to accelerate their wealth-building efforts.

As discussed in *The Unstoppable Road to Wealth Creation*, *The Things Wealthy People Do*, and *The Mind of a Trillionaire*, financial knowledge is more than just a tool—it is a weapon in the fight for financial success. By acquiring and applying this knowledge, you can separate yourself from the average and position yourself for lasting wealth. It's not enough to hope for success; you must arm yourself with the knowledge to make it happen.

Chapter 6:

Crafting a Wealth-Oriented Lifestyle

In the pursuit of wealth, many individuals overlook an essential aspect: lifestyle. Wealth isn't just about accumulating money—it's about the choices you make every single day that ultimately determine your financial future. The decisions you make about how you spend your time, manage your money, and structure your life all play a pivotal role in your ability to build lasting wealth. Crafting a wealth-oriented lifestyle is an ongoing process, but by aligning your daily actions with your long-term financial goals, you can steadily pave the path to success.

In this chapter, I'll draw on insights from *The Unstoppable Road to Wealth Creation*, *The Things Wealthy People Do*, and *The Mind of a Trillionaire* to show you how to align your lifestyle with your financial ambitions. From time management to financial habits to decision-making, we'll explore the small changes you can make that will compound over time, creating a life of wealth and prosperity.

The Foundation of a Wealth-Oriented Lifestyle

A wealth-oriented lifestyle is not just about being frugal or cutting back on luxuries; it's about making conscious choices that align with long-term success. This involves developing a mindset that views money and resources as tools to achieve greater goals, rather than ends in themselves. The wealthy understand that money must be managed and leveraged to build something larger—a legacy, a business, or even a network that perpetuates wealth for generations to come.

The foundation of this lifestyle begins with understanding that wealth is as much about *how* you live as it is about *what* you accumulate. As discussed in *The Unstoppable Road to Wealth Creation*, wealth-building is a strategic endeavor that requires more than just luck or hard work. It requires intentionality in how you organize your life, prioritize your time, and invest your resources.

Time Management: The Ultimate Wealth Resource

Time is arguably the most valuable asset we have, and it's the one thing we can never get back. In *The Things Wealthy People Do*, I discuss how the wealthiest individuals understand the importance of time management. They don't just prioritize their financial goals—they prioritize their time. Wealthy individuals guard their time like it's the most precious commodity because they understand its power in the wealth-building process.

Illustrative Example:

Consider someone like Warren Buffett, whose entire career has been built on deliberate decision-making and time management. Buffett's daily schedule is tightly structured around focused work, reading, and contemplation—activities that feed his knowledge and understanding of business. His wealth is a direct reflection of the years spent making wise decisions with his time.

The truth is, time is often wasted on activities that don't add value to our financial goals—whether it's mindless television consumption, excessive social media browsing, or socializing without purpose. In contrast, wealth-oriented individuals are deliberate in how they allocate their time. This means choosing to spend time learning new skills, networking with valuable contacts, or working toward their financial goals.

Actionable Tip:

Start by creating a time audit. Track how you spend your time for a week, noting how much time is dedicated to activities that directly support your financial aspirations. Is your time being used to its highest potential? Are there areas where you can cut back on non-productive activities and redirect that time to wealth-building actions?

Financial Habits: Small Decisions with Big Impact

As I've detailed in *The Unstoppable Road to Wealth Creation*, financial success is largely the result of small, consistent decisions that compound over time. These decisions include how you save, invest, and manage your money on a day-to-day basis. In fact, the most successful individuals are often those who cultivate healthy financial habits, like saving a percentage of their income, paying attention to their spending, and continuously reinvesting in their growth.

In *The Mind of a Trillionaire*, I share how billionaires like Jeff Bezos and Elon Musk have built their fortunes by not only focusing on big business decisions but by managing the day-to-day financial aspects of their lives with discipline. They understand that every small action—whether it's limiting unnecessary spending or making wise investment choices—plays a part in creating the financial freedom they enjoy today.

Illustrative Example:

Let's take the example of Elon Musk's investment philosophy. Musk often reinvests much of his earnings from ventures like Tesla and SpaceX back into his businesses, focusing on long-term goals rather than short-term gains. While this may seem like a sacrifice to the average person, Musk understands that by redirecting resources into areas of potential growth, he is positioning himself for monumental financial success in the future.

The average person, in contrast, might focus more on short-term gratification, spending money on luxuries that don't contribute to their long-term wealth. Crafting a wealth-oriented lifestyle requires you to reframe these habits and make financial decisions that serve your long-term objectives.

Actionable Tip:

Review your monthly spending. Look for patterns that are not aligned with your financial goals. Are there areas where you can cut back and invest those savings into your wealth-building endeavors? Whether it's cutting down on dining out or investing in a savings plan, small shifts in your financial habits can have a significant impact over time.

Networking and Relationships: The Power of Surrounding Yourself with the Right People

In *The Things Wealthy People Do*, I emphasize the importance of relationships in wealth-building. Wealth is not built in isolation, and the wealthiest people in the world are often those who are surrounded by individuals who challenge them, encourage them, and provide valuable insights. Networking with like-minded individuals who share your vision can dramatically accelerate your wealth-building process.

Illustrative Example:

Take Richard Branson, the founder of Virgin Group, as an example. Branson has always made networking a priority, surrounding himself with a diverse group of individuals—from entrepreneurs to thought leaders to experts in various industries. By learning from others and exchanging ideas, Branson was able to scale his businesses and build a global empire. This is a testament to how relationships can become powerful tools for success.

In contrast, individuals who isolate themselves or fail to cultivate strong relationships often find themselves stuck in limiting environments, which can hinder progress. Building a strong network and seeking out mentorship are powerful components of a wealth-oriented lifestyle.

Actionable Tip:

Make a list of individuals who have supported your growth and success so far. Consider how you can nurture these relationships or expand your network by connecting with new, influential individuals who align with your financial goals. Attend events, conferences, or engage in online communities that focus on wealth-building and personal development.

Health and Wellness: The Silent Contributor to Financial Success

A wealth-oriented lifestyle goes beyond just financial decisions—it also includes taking care of your health. After all, what is wealth if you don't have the energy or the well-being to enjoy it? In *The Unstoppable Road to Wealth Creation*, I emphasize that building wealth requires a mindset of long-term thinking, and that includes taking care of your physical health. Wealthy individuals know that they must maintain peak physical and mental performance in order to tackle the challenges that come with managing substantial wealth.

Illustrative Example:

Oprah Winfrey is an example of someone who understands the

connection between health and success. Despite her grueling schedule, Oprah prioritizes health and wellness, incorporating fitness routines, healthy eating habits, and mindfulness practices into her life. Her focus on health ensures she remains sharp, energetic, and able to manage her empire effectively.

Actionable Tip:

Evaluate your current lifestyle choices regarding health. Are you getting enough exercise? Are you eating in ways that support your long-term health and energy levels? Begin implementing small, sustainable changes that prioritize both your mental and physical well-being. A wealth-oriented lifestyle requires you to operate at your best—and that starts with taking care of yourself.

Crafting a Wealth-Oriented Routine: Consistency is Key

Wealth-building isn't about a single, bold decision; it's about consistently making the right decisions day in and day out. In *The Mind of a Trillionaire*, I discuss how billionaires and entrepreneurs create routines that align with their long-term financial goals. From setting daily priorities to tracking progress, wealth-oriented individuals cultivate routines that help them stay focused on their financial objectives.

Incorporating wealth-building actions into your daily routine—whether it's setting aside time for reading, saving a percentage of your income, or networking with key people—can lead to compounded results over time.

Actionable Tip:

Create a daily checklist that includes actions you can take to build your wealth. This might include reviewing your financial goals, reading a financial article, making an investment decision, or learning a new skill. Over time, these small actions will add up to significant progress.

Conclusion: Living Wealthily Every Day

A wealth-oriented lifestyle is more than just a series of decisions—it's a mindset and a set of practices that align with your long-term goals. By consciously deciding to live in a way that supports your financial ambitions, you will begin to see compounded results in your wealth and overall success. Time management, financial habits, networking, health, and consistency all work together to create a lifestyle that fosters growth and prosperity.

In *The Unstoppable Road to Wealth Creation, The Things Wealthy People Do*, and *The Mind of a Trillionaire*, we explore the various ways you can align your life with the principles of financial success. By crafting a wealth-oriented lifestyle, you are positioning yourself for lasting success, not just financially, but also in every area of your life.

Chapter 7:

The Influence of Vision on Wealth Creation

In the journey of wealth creation, one fundamental element often separates the successful from the average: vision. Without a clear and compelling vision, financial success can feel like a distant, uncertain goal. Vision serves as the blueprint, the driving force that directs all your efforts, choices, and actions. It isn't just a mere wish or dream—it's a detailed and actionable plan for where you want to go and how you're going to get there.

As I explored in *The Unstoppable Road to Wealth Creation*, the process of wealth building is not random, nor is it left to chance. The most successful people in the world didn't just stumble upon their wealth—they envisioned it long before they began their journey. Similarly, in *The Things Wealthy People Do*, we learn that wealth-building is intentional, and every great financial success story starts with a vision that guides every step. And in *The Mind of a Trillionaire*, I examined the power of long-term thinking and visionary leadership, showing that without a deep sense of purpose and direction, even the most talented individuals can struggle to create lasting wealth.

In this chapter, we will explore how developing a crystal-clear vision for your financial future not only provides you with direction, but also serves as a constant motivator, especially during challenging times. Your vision will shape your decisions, inform your actions, and become the bedrock of your financial plan.

Understanding Vision: The Fuel Behind Wealth Creation

Vision is more than just a goal; it is a mental picture of your desired future. It acts as a guiding light in the darkness of uncertainty, giving you a sense of purpose and urgency. But vision alone is not enough—what matters is the clarity of your vision. The more specific, detailed, and vivid it is, the more likely it will drive you to take the necessary steps to turn it into reality.

A clear vision is the first step toward any meaningful achievement. This vision becomes the foundation upon which every decision and every action is built. Whether it's choosing the right investment opportunities or deciding on the next business venture, your vision will be your compass.

Illustrative Example:

Consider someone like Bill Gates, whose vision for technology and computing in the 1970s transformed the landscape of modern business. Gates didn't just want to make money—he wanted to empower people through software. His vision of making a computer in every home and on every desk led him to establish Microsoft, a company that has since grown to become one of the largest and most successful in the world. His vision was clear, compelling, and directed his actions, even when faced with numerous obstacles.

The Role of Vision in Financial Motivation

Vision plays an important role in fueling motivation. Financial success is not a straight path; it is often filled with obstacles, setbacks, and challenges. During difficult times, a strong vision can provide the motivation needed to continue working toward your goals.

In *The Unstoppable Road to Wealth Creation*, I discuss the importance of perseverance in the face of adversity. One key factor that helps individuals persevere is the strength of their vision. When the road gets tough, it's the vision that keeps you going. It's the image of your future success that helps you push through challenges and stay focused on the bigger picture. Vision gives you a reason to keep going when it feels easier to quit.

Illustrative Example:

Consider Thomas Edison, the inventor of the light bulb. Edison faced countless failures in his quest to create the first commercially viable light bulb. Yet, through it all, his vision of a world illuminated by electricity kept him going. He didn't see failure as the end, but as part of the process. His vision was so compelling that it gave him the strength to overcome 1,000 unsuccessful attempts to find the right filament. Ultimately, his persistence paid off, and his vision came to life, changing the world forever.

Vision and Clarity: The Power of Specificity

A vision without clarity is just a vague idea. In *The Things Wealthy People Do*, I explain that wealthy individuals do not just have an idea of success—they have a detailed, specific picture of what that success looks like. The clearer and more detailed your vision, the more power it holds. Specificity is key because it helps direct your efforts and minimizes distractions.

For instance, a person who simply says, "I want to be rich" is unlikely to experience the same level of focus and drive as someone who says, "I want to build a $10 million business in the next 10 years by investing in real estate and technology." The second vision is not only more specific, but it also includes a timeline and a plan of action. This clarity helps break down a seemingly impossible goal into manageable, actionable steps.

Actionable Tip:

Start by writing down your financial vision in as much detail as possible. Include specifics about how much wealth you want to create, by when, and through what means. Your vision should feel vivid and exciting, painting a clear picture of the lifestyle you want to lead. Break your larger vision down into smaller, more manageable goals, and develop a strategy to bring them to life.

Vision as the Foundation of Your Financial Plan

A well-developed vision isn't just a motivating force—it's the foundation of your financial plan. Your vision informs the way you allocate your resources, choose investments, and approach financial risks. It allows you to filter out distractions and stay focused on what truly matters.

In *The Mind of a Trillionaire*, I delve into how the wealthiest individuals structure their financial plans around their vision. For example, Elon Musk's vision of making humanity a multi-planetary species has driven his investments in space exploration, energy, and electric vehicles. His financial decisions are directly tied to his larger vision, and his success is a reflection of that alignment.

Similarly, when you develop a clear vision, you are able to make smarter, more strategic financial decisions that align with your long-term goals. Rather than making impulsive investments or spending recklessly, you'll be guided by the bigger picture, ensuring that every move you make brings you closer to your vision.

Illustrative Example:

A powerful example of vision influencing financial decisions can be seen in Warren Buffett's investment strategy. Buffett's vision of investing in businesses with strong fundamentals and long-term potential has led him to acquire companies like Coca-Cola and Geico. He isn't focused on short-term gains; he is building a legacy of wealth based on his vision of owning businesses that will continue to thrive for generations. His financial decisions are rooted in the clarity of his vision.

Creating and Refining Your Vision

Creating a vision isn't a one-time event. It's an ongoing process that requires regular refinement. As you grow, learn, and experience new things, your vision may evolve. Successful individuals constantly refine their vision, ensuring it stays aligned with their changing goals and circumstances. This adaptability is crucial for continued financial growth.

Actionable Tip:

Set aside time every few months to review and refine your vision. Ask yourself: Has anything changed in your financial goals or priorities? Are there new opportunities or obstacles that need to be considered? Regularly revisiting your vision ensures that you stay on track and adapt to the changing circumstances of life.

Vision and the Power of Belief

Vision also plays a crucial role in developing belief. Belief in the possibility of achieving your financial goals is essential. Without belief, your vision will remain nothing more than a fantasy. In *The Unstoppable Road to Wealth Creation*, I discuss the importance of having unshakable faith in your ability to achieve your vision. This belief fuels your determination, even when faced with setbacks.

When you truly believe in the possibility of your vision, you are willing to take risks, make sacrifices, and do whatever it takes to turn that vision into a reality. The belief in your vision drives your actions and gives you the resilience needed to overcome challenges.

Illustrative Example:

Take Oprah Winfrey's story. As a young woman, Oprah had a vision of becoming a media mogul, despite facing immense challenges and societal obstacles. Her belief in her vision kept her moving forward, and she ultimately achieved it, becoming one of the most influential women in the world. Her story is a testament to the power of belief and vision in the pursuit of wealth.

Conclusion: Vision as Your North Star

In this chapter, we have explored how vision plays an instrumental role in wealth creation. A clear, compelling vision provides direction, motivation, and clarity, and serves as the foundation for every financial decision you make. Whether you're building a business, investing in assets, or planning for long-term financial security, your vision will guide you every step of the way.

Remember that vision is not a one-time exercise—it is an ongoing process that requires refinement and belief. By aligning your financial plan with your vision and staying true to your larger goals, you are setting yourself up for lasting wealth and success.

In the end, a well-crafted vision is not just about financial wealth—it's about creating the life you desire. It's about using your financial resources to build a legacy, achieve your dreams, and make an impact on the world. The journey of wealth creation is not just about the money—it's about creating a vision that drives you to live your most fulfilling life.

Section 2:

The Strategy for Financial Growth (Methods & Systems)

Chapter 8:

Generating Multiple Income Streams

In the modern financial landscape, relying on a single income stream is not only limiting but also risky. The financial environment is increasingly volatile, with job security no longer a guaranteed promise, and the market continuously evolving. In this context, building multiple income streams has become a crucial strategy for those seeking not only to survive but thrive financially.

Throughout *The Unstoppable Road to Wealth Creation*, I emphasize the importance of diversification as a cornerstone of financial security. Wealthy individuals understand that the key to long-term prosperity lies in the ability to generate income from different sources. The more income streams you have, the less dependent you become on any one of them, and the more resilient your financial portfolio becomes in the face of economic uncertainty.

In *The Things Wealthy People Do*, I explored the habits of financially successful people. One of the most consistent traits among the wealthy is their ability to leverage multiple sources of income. From passive investments to active side hustles, they understand that diversified income streams are the backbone of financial freedom. In *The Mind of a Trillionaire*, I further explore how the wealthiest individuals, including billionaires, build vast financial empires by generating income from a variety of sources. They do not just rely on their primary business or investments but strategically position themselves across multiple industries to maximize wealth-building opportunities.

In this chapter, we'll take an in-depth look at how to generate multiple income streams. We'll cover various avenues to consider, from traditional investments in stocks and real estate to newer sources like digital businesses and passive income. The key to building true wealth is not putting all your eggs in one basket, and by the end of this chapter, you will have a clearer understanding of how to create a robust portfolio of income streams to support your financial goals.

The Power of Diversification in Income

The concept of diversification is a powerful tool in wealth-building. When you rely on a single source of income—such as a job, a single business, or one investment—you expose yourself to unnecessary risks. What happens if your job disappears or your business faces a downturn? What happens if the market crashes, or a single investment fails? The absence of diversification means that a single setback could threaten your financial stability.

Illustrative Example:

Take the case of many individuals who were heavily reliant on their primary job during the 2008 financial crisis. Millions lost their jobs, homes, and savings because they had not diversified their income. Contrast that with individuals who had diversified income streams through investments, side businesses, or passive income, many of whom were able to weather the storm and continue growing their wealth even during a downturn.

By contrast, wealthy individuals spread their financial risk across multiple assets and income sources. In doing so, they increase the likelihood that their overall financial situation will remain strong, regardless of the ups and downs in any one sector.

Types of Income Streams to Consider

Let's now look at some of the most common types of income streams and how you can build them. Each of these offers unique advantages and challenges, but the key is to choose a variety that aligns with your financial goals and risk tolerance.

1. Active Income

Active income is earned through the direct exchange of time and effort. This is the most common form of income—salaries, wages, freelance work, or the income earned from running a business.

Example:

Consider the income you generate from your primary business. In *The Unstoppable Road to Wealth Creation*, I explain that starting a business is one of the most powerful ways to build wealth, as it creates not only a source of active income but also the foundation for potential passive income streams later on. For instance, if you start a business that generates $10,000 per month, that is active income. However, you can later transform it into a passive income stream by hiring managers to run the business for you or by automating processes.

2. Passive Income

Unlike active income, passive income allows you to earn money without continuously working for it. It comes from investments or assets that generate revenue over time, such as dividends from stocks, rental income from real estate, royalties from books, and income from digital products.

Example:

In *The Things Wealthy People Do*, I share the story of a successful real estate investor who was able to retire early by building a portfolio of rental properties that generated consistent monthly income. In this case, the investor did the work upfront by purchasing and managing the properties, but the income they received was passive, meaning they didn't need to work actively to generate it. Once the properties were set up, the rental payments rolled in every month without them having to work for each payment.

For example, renting out properties, as described in *The Mind of a Trillionaire*, offers the opportunity for passive income once the properties are purchased. As with any passive income stream, the setup can be intensive at first, but over time, you begin to benefit from steady income without actively engaging in daily work.

3. Investment Income

Investments in stocks, bonds, mutual funds, and exchange-traded funds (ETFs) can yield returns in the form of interest, dividends, and capital gains. This is a crucial income stream for anyone aiming to build wealth. However, it requires a strong understanding of market principles and the ability to select investments that will provide long-term returns.

Example:

Warren Buffett, whose story I highlighted in *The Unstoppable Road to Wealth Creation*, is one of the most famous investors in the world. His wealth is largely derived from making strategic investments in companies with strong fundamentals. His investment strategy centers on buying shares of companies that will generate profits and pay dividends for years to come.

If you decide to invest in stocks, start by building a diversified portfolio of high-quality companies, mutual funds, or ETFs that fit your risk tolerance. If managed properly, investment income can grow exponentially over time, allowing you to earn returns on your returns.

4. Side Hustles

Side hustles have become a significant source of income for many individuals. A side hustle is a job or business you do outside of your primary source of income. It's often something you can start with little capital and can scale over time. With the advent of the digital age, side hustles are more accessible than ever.

Example:

In *The Mind of a Trillionaire*, I explore the stories of successful individuals who started small side businesses before turning them into multimillion-dollar enterprises. Take the example of a digital entrepreneur who begins with a small e-commerce store and later scales it into a global brand. What started as a side hustle can quickly turn into a significant source of income. Many people today are building their wealth through side hustles like dropshipping, affiliate marketing, and freelance digital services.

5. Royalties and Licensing

Royalties and licensing provide an excellent avenue for passive income. This form of income is generated when you create something—such as a book, music, patent, or software—and license it to others for a fee.

Example:

In *The Things Wealthy People Do*, I discussed how some of the wealthiest people in the world earn royalties from their creative works. For instance, authors and musicians receive royalty payments every time their books or songs are sold or licensed. As an entrepreneur, you can earn income by licensing your intellectual property to other businesses or individuals.

6. Digital Businesses

The rise of the internet and digital platforms has opened up countless opportunities for generating income online. Digital businesses range from e-commerce, online courses, and digital marketing to content creation on platforms like YouTube, Instagram, and TikTok. The beauty of digital businesses is that they can scale quickly and generate significant income with relatively low upfront costs.

Example:

Take the example of a content creator who builds a large following on social media platforms. Once a substantial audience is established, the creator can generate income through sponsored content, affiliate marketing, and advertising. In *The Mind of a Trillionaire*, I explain how digital entrepreneurs have rapidly scaled businesses from small startups to global enterprises using social media and e-commerce tools.

The Power of Compounding Income Streams

The more income streams you have, the greater the potential for wealth accumulation. It's not just about having multiple sources of income—it's about creating an ecosystem where these streams work together and build upon each other. This concept is what I refer to as "compounding income streams" in *The Unstoppable Road to Wealth Creation*. When one income stream grows, it can help fund the expansion of others.

For example, income from a rental property can be reinvested into stocks, which can then generate dividends. These dividends can be used to fund a new side hustle or further investment in real estate. Over time, this compounding effect can lead to exponential wealth accumulation.

Conclusion

Building multiple income streams is one of the most effective strategies for achieving financial security and long-term wealth. By diversifying your sources of income, you reduce risk, increase opportunities, and create a resilient financial portfolio. Whether it's through active income, passive income, investments, or digital ventures, each income stream you build adds a layer of security to your financial life.

As discussed throughout *The Unstoppable Road to Wealth Creation*, *The Things Wealthy People Do*, and *The Mind of a Trillionaire*, wealthy individuals understand that their financial success is tied to their ability to generate income from various sources. They do not rely on one stream but instead create a web of income opportunities that allow them to grow their wealth over time.

By strategically choosing the right income streams, diversifying your investments, and leveraging the power of compounding, you can ensure that your financial future is not only secure but thriving. The key to wealth creation is to start now, take action, and continuously build on your progress.

Chapter 9:

Scaling a Business for Long-Term Prosperity

Scaling a business is one of the most profound ways to accelerate wealth creation. A small business with the right approach can evolve into a highly profitable, long-term venture capable of generating wealth for its owners, employees, and stakeholders. However, scaling isn't something that happens by accident. It requires strategy, commitment, and a clear understanding of how to move from a simple operation to a business that generates substantial profits and supports sustainable growth. In this chapter, we'll break down the key elements of scaling a business and provide actionable steps for turning your business into a wealth-generating powerhouse.

In my previous book, *The Unstoppable Road to Wealth Creation*, I discussed the fundamental importance of starting a business as a path to creating wealth. However, starting a business is only the first step. As we delve deeper into the idea of scaling, we will explore how to expand a successful small venture into a thriving company that generates exponential financial growth.

In *The Things Wealthy People Do*, I highlighted how the wealthiest individuals manage their businesses and investments with the goal of creating lasting success. A key takeaway from that book was how these individuals approach scaling: they never settle for small gains. Instead, they systematically put in place the right infrastructure, technology, and talent to grow their businesses into major players in their respective industries. In *The Mind of a Trillionaire*, I discussed billionaires who began with small ventures, but through careful scaling, they created empires. The fundamental principle underlying all successful business growth is a strategy that aims for long-term prosperity.

Scaling a business is not simply about increasing revenue; it's about building systems that can handle and sustain growth while maintaining or improving profitability. In this chapter, we will dive into the core principles of scaling a business effectively and provide a roadmap to move from a small-scale operation to a business powerhouse.

1. The Mindset for Scaling a Business

The first step in scaling a business is understanding that it requires a shift in mindset. Many small business owners are used to managing every aspect of their operation, from customer service to finance to operations. However, when you aim to scale your business, you must transition from a one-person operation to an enterprise that can operate efficiently without your constant involvement in every detail. This shift is essential for growth, and it begins with a mindset that embraces delegation, systems, and long-term thinking.

In *The Unstoppable Road to Wealth Creation*, I discussed the importance of mindset in entrepreneurship. To create a business that scales successfully, you must think beyond short-term profits and consider the systems, strategies, and structures required to support exponential growth. This mindset is often what separates business owners who plateau from those who achieve massive success.

Illustrative Example:

Take the example of Amazon. Jeff Bezos started Amazon as a small online bookstore out of his garage, but he quickly realized that to scale, he needed to think beyond his own capacity to handle operations. Bezos focused on creating systems that allowed Amazon to grow rapidly while maintaining efficiency. From investing in technology to implementing customer service strategies that could scale globally, Bezos was always thinking about the infrastructure that would allow his business to expand seamlessly.

2. Systematizing Business Processes

One of the most important components of scaling a business is systematizing your operations. In the early stages, a business owner may be able to handle everything manually. However, as the business grows, manual processes become inefficient and unsustainable. Successful business owners recognize this need for systems early on and take steps to implement processes that can handle increased demand.

Key Areas to Systematize:

- **Operations:** From inventory management to order fulfillment, systematizing your operations ensures that your business can handle large volumes of customers without sacrificing quality.

- **Customer Service:** Whether it's through automation, customer support software, or outsourcing, creating efficient systems to manage customer service inquiries allows you to scale without becoming overwhelmed.

- **Marketing:** Automation tools and digital marketing strategies allow businesses to scale their marketing efforts, reaching more customers while maintaining a consistent message.

In *The Things Wealthy People Do*, I emphasized that systems allow business owners to shift from working in the business to working on the business. It's no longer about managing day-to-day tasks, but about building a scalable infrastructure that works independently of your direct involvement.

Illustrative Example:

Take the example of a small online retailer that started by selling hand-made jewelry. Initially, the business owner was responsible for everything, from making the jewelry to packaging orders and responding to customer emails. However, as the business grew, the owner realized that to scale, they needed to implement systems. They hired additional staff to handle production, implemented a customer service system with a response template, and used e-commerce automation tools to handle orders and inventory. This allowed the business to handle a much larger volume of sales without compromising on quality or customer satisfaction.

3. Building a Strong Team

As you scale, the need for a talented, reliable team becomes paramount. While you may start out as a one-person operation, the only way to successfully scale is to hire and empower others to take on various roles within your business. This might mean hiring full-time employees, outsourcing tasks, or even building a team of independent contractors, depending on your business model.

In *The Mind of a Trillionaire*, I discussed how billionaires like Elon Musk have built large teams around them to help scale their businesses. They understand that scaling requires more than just capital—it requires skilled people who can manage different aspects of the operation. Successful entrepreneurs invest time in building a great team and delegate responsibility to trusted individuals who can help the business grow.

Illustrative Example:

When Facebook first launched, Mark Zuckerberg was involved in every aspect of the company. However, as Facebook grew, he realized that to scale, he needed to hire talented engineers, marketers, and managers who could take on specific tasks. As Facebook expanded globally, Zuckerberg's ability to delegate responsibility was essential to the company's success. In his case, hiring the right talent was not just about filling positions; it was about finding people who could contribute to the vision of the company and drive long-term growth.

4. Expanding Your Customer Base

As you scale, attracting and retaining customers becomes a key priority. A business can only grow as fast as its customer base expands. However, scaling your customer acquisition strategies can be challenging. It's not enough to rely on word-of-mouth or organic growth—businesses need to actively pursue new customers through a variety of channels.

Key Strategies for Customer Base Expansion:

- **Digital Marketing:** Utilizing tools like SEO, paid advertising, and social media can help you reach new customers on a global scale.

- **Referral Programs:** Encouraging existing customers to refer friends and family can significantly expand your customer base.

- **Partnerships and Collaborations:** Collaborating with other businesses or influencers in your industry can help you tap into new audiences.

In *The Things Wealthy People Do*, I discussed how successful entrepreneurs invest heavily in marketing and partnerships to grow their customer base. The key is to understand who your ideal customer is and tailor your marketing efforts to target them effectively.

Illustrative Example:

Consider the case of a small business owner who operates an online fitness coaching service. Initially, the business grew through word-of-mouth referrals, but the owner realized that to scale, they needed to reach more people. The owner invested in digital marketing by running targeted

Facebook ads, worked with influencers in the fitness industry to promote their services, and launched a referral program to encourage current customers to recommend friends. These strategies helped the business expand its customer base exponentially.

5. Managing Cash Flow and Financial Planning

As your business grows, managing cash flow becomes increasingly important. The financial demands of a scaling business can be substantial, and without careful planning, you can run into cash flow problems that can stifle growth. It's important to manage your finances wisely, from securing working capital to investing in growth opportunities.

In *The Unstoppable Road to Wealth Creation*, I discussed how proper financial planning is critical for business success. Successful scaling doesn't just require capital—it requires a well-thought-out financial strategy that ensures you can reinvest profits into the business while maintaining enough liquidity to cover expenses.

Illustrative Example:

A small software company begins to scale and needs to hire more developers, invest in marketing, and expand its operations. The owner realizes that managing cash flow is essential to ensuring the business doesn't run into financial trouble. By securing a line of credit and carefully planning expenses, the company is able to reinvest profits into growth opportunities without running out of cash. This careful financial management allows the company to continue scaling at a sustainable pace.

6. Leveraging Technology for Growth

In today's business environment, technology plays a critical role in scaling. Whether it's automating processes, managing inventory, or reaching customers through digital channels, technology can help you streamline operations, reduce costs, and increase efficiency. Leveraging the right tools and systems is often the key to scaling effectively.

In *The Mind of a Trillionaire*, I discussed how technology has been a game-changer for billionaires like Bill Gates and Jeff Bezos, who have used technological advancements to scale their businesses globally. Whether it's through cloud computing, e-commerce platforms, or advanced analytics, technology enables businesses to scale faster and more efficiently than ever before.

Illustrative Example:

A retail business that started with a physical store can leverage e-commerce platforms, automated inventory management systems, and digital marketing tools to expand its reach to customers around the world. By utilizing these technologies, the business can scale its operations far beyond what would have been possible with a physical store alone.

Conclusion: The Path to Long-Term Prosperity

Scaling a business is an exciting and challenging process that requires strategic thinking, systematization, and careful planning. As discussed throughout *The Unstoppable Road to Wealth Creation*, *The Things Wealthy People Do*, and *The Mind of a Trillionaire*, successful entrepreneurs don't just focus on short-term success—they plan for long-term prosperity by building businesses that can grow sustainably.

By shifting your mindset, systematizing processes, hiring the right team, expanding your customer base, and leveraging technology, you can transform a small business into a thriving, wealth-generating enterprise. The key is to remain focused on the long-term vision while continuously refining your business strategies to drive growth.

Building a business that scales takes time, effort, and resources, but with the right approach, it's one of the most effective ways to generate lasting wealth. It's not just about working harder—it's about working smarter, building systems that work for you, and positioning your business for long-term success. The road to scaling is challenging, but it's also incredibly rewarding. And with the right strategy in place, you can create a business that thrives for years to come.

Chapter 10:

Smart Investment Strategies for Sustainable Growth

Investment is one of the most powerful ways to build lasting wealth. It is through wise investing that individuals and businesses can generate income, preserve capital, and grow their wealth over time. Yet, investing isn't about merely putting money into random opportunities; it requires a strategy, discipline, and a keen understanding of risk and return. In this chapter, we will dive deep into smart investment strategies that contribute to long-term sustainable growth. We will explore key areas of investment, such as asset allocation, real estate investing, and the importance of building a diverse portfolio. Additionally, we will discuss how to make informed, strategic decisions that align with both your risk tolerance and long-term financial goals.

This chapter draws inspiration from the core principles of wealth creation discussed in *The Unstoppable Road to Wealth Creation*, where the importance of disciplined financial management is emphasized. Similarly, *The Things Wealthy People Do* sheds light on the mindset of the affluent when it comes to investment, while *The Mind of a Trillionaire* examines how billionaires approach investing. Here, we'll draw on these concepts to guide you in making investment decisions that ensure sustainable wealth growth.

1. The Power of Asset Allocation

Asset allocation is one of the most important concepts when it comes to investing. It refers to how an investor divides their investment portfolio among different asset categories, such as stocks, bonds, real estate, and cash equivalents. The principle behind asset allocation is simple: by spreading your investments across different types of assets, you can mitigate risk and enhance the potential for returns.

In *The Unstoppable Road to Wealth Creation*, I emphasized how understanding the balance between risk and return is crucial to building wealth. Successful investors do not put all their eggs in one basket; instead, they diversify their investments to ensure that their portfolio is resilient to market fluctuations.

Key Asset Classes:

- **Stocks:** Equities are typically the highest-yielding asset class over the long term but come with higher volatility.
- **Bonds:** Bonds provide stable returns and act as a hedge against stock market volatility. They are typically safer than stocks, though with lower returns.

- **Real Estate:** Real estate investments, whether through direct property ownership or real estate investment trusts (REITs), offer strong potential for wealth growth, passive income, and capital appreciation.

- **Commodities:** Assets like gold, oil, or agricultural products can serve as a hedge against inflation and economic downturns.

- **Cash and Cash Equivalents:** While cash may seem like a conservative investment, having liquidity ensures that investors can take advantage of opportunities when they arise.

In *The Things Wealthy People Do*, I shared how wealthy individuals typically maintain a balanced asset allocation, adjusting it as they approach specific financial goals. By maintaining an asset mix that aligns with their risk tolerance, these individuals can manage volatility and enhance their chances for long-term financial growth.

Illustrative Example:

Consider an investor with a balanced portfolio consisting of 60% stocks, 30% bonds, and 10% real estate. During a market downturn, the stock market may experience a significant loss, but the bond investments would provide a steady stream of income, and the real estate portion may remain stable or even appreciate. This diversification reduces the investor's overall risk while allowing them to capture the growth potential of stocks and real estate.

2. Real Estate Investing for Long-Term Wealth

Real estate has long been regarded as one of the safest and most lucrative investment vehicles. In *The Unstoppable Road to Wealth Creation*, I highlighted the importance of understanding the dynamics of the real estate market and using it as a tool to build wealth. Whether through direct property ownership, real estate investment trusts (REITs), or property flipping, real estate investing offers several opportunities to generate passive income, build equity, and grow wealth.

Real estate investments can provide several benefits, including:

- **Cash Flow:** Rental properties generate consistent monthly income.
- **Appreciation:** Over time, real estate tends to appreciate in value, adding to the wealth of the investor.
- **Tax Advantages:** Real estate investors often benefit from tax deductions, such as mortgage interest and depreciation.
- **Leverage:** Real estate is a unique asset in that it allows you to use leverage (borrowed capital) to finance the purchase of property, potentially magnifying your return on investment.

In *The Mind of a Trillionaire*, I analyzed the investment strategies of successful billionaires, many of whom have built significant portions of their wealth through real estate. Real estate is not just about buying properties but about understanding the broader market trends and identifying high-potential areas for investment.

Illustrative Example:

Consider an investor who purchases a rental property in an emerging neighborhood where property values are expected to rise. The investor finances the purchase with a mortgage, allowing them to leverage their capital. Over time, the property appreciates in value, and the investor also generates passive income from rent. By the time the property is sold, the investor has made a substantial profit, both from appreciation and rental income.

3. Building a Diverse Portfolio

A diverse portfolio is crucial for reducing risk while enhancing the potential for growth. In *The Unstoppable Road to Wealth Creation*, I discussed how a diverse investment approach allows investors to weather the ups and downs of different market sectors. A diversified portfolio spreads risk across various asset classes, reducing the impact of volatility in any single investment.

Types of Diversification:

- **Geographic Diversification:** Investing in different regions or countries can mitigate risk, as economic cycles vary from one place to another.

- **Sector Diversification:** Spreading investments across various industries (e.g., technology, healthcare, real estate, energy) ensures that a downturn in one sector does not severely impact the entire portfolio.

- **Investment Type Diversification:** Combining different investment types, such as stocks, bonds, real estate, and commodities, further balances risk and opportunity.

In *The Things Wealthy People Do*, I provided examples of how wealthier individuals often diversify not only within asset classes but across asset classes, balancing high-risk investments like stocks with safer investments like bonds or real estate.

Illustrative Example:

An investor could create a diversified portfolio by allocating 50% to a mix of stocks, 20% to real estate, 20% to bonds, and 10% to commodities. During an economic downturn, the stocks may lose value, but the real estate holdings may remain stable, and the bond investments may offer a steady income. This diversity ensures that the investor's wealth continues to grow, regardless of market conditions.

4. Strategic Investment in Stocks and Bonds

Stocks and bonds are two of the most commonly used investment vehicles. Stocks offer the potential for high returns, but they also carry a higher risk. Bonds, on the other hand, are typically safer but offer lower returns. Smart investors understand how to balance these two asset types in a way that maximizes returns while minimizing risk.

In *The Mind of a Trillionaire*, we examined how some of the wealthiest people in the world use both stocks and bonds in their portfolios. While stocks offer long-term growth potential, bonds provide stability and income during periods of market volatility.

Illustrative Example:

An investor with a 70% allocation to stocks and a 30% allocation to bonds could achieve a balance between risk and return. In times of market growth, the stock portion of the portfolio would appreciate significantly. During a market downturn, the bond portion of the portfolio would provide stability and help offset the losses from the stock market.

5. Alternative Investments and Passive Income Streams

In addition to traditional investments, alternative investments are becoming increasingly popular among investors seeking to diversify their portfolios. These can include private equity, hedge funds, venture capital, and collectibles such as art, wine, or rare cars.

In *The Unstoppable Road to Wealth Creation*, I explored the idea of creating multiple income streams to ensure financial security. Alternative investments offer unique opportunities for generating passive income and building wealth. By investing in assets that are not correlated with the stock market, investors can protect their portfolios from market volatility.

Illustrative Example:

A high-net-worth individual may invest in a venture capital fund that targets early-stage tech startups. While this investment carries significant risk, it also offers the potential for high returns if the startups succeed. The investor could complement this with investments in real estate and stocks, balancing the high risk of venture capital with more stable investments in traditional asset classes.

6. Risk Management and Mitigation

Every investment carries a degree of risk. However, successful investors understand how to mitigate these risks through various strategies. In *The Mind of a Trillionaire*, I analyzed how billionaires manage risk—whether through diversification, hedging, or using financial instruments such as options and futures to protect their investments.

Key Risk Management Strategies:

- **Diversification:** As mentioned, diversification across asset classes, sectors, and geographies is one of the best ways to reduce risk.

- **Hedging:** Investors use hedging strategies, such as options, to protect against downside risk in their portfolios.

- **Risk Tolerance:** Understanding your risk tolerance is crucial. Some investors may be comfortable with higher risk for the potential of greater rewards, while others may prefer a more conservative approach.

In *The Things Wealthy People Do*, we saw that many wealthy individuals conduct extensive due diligence before making an investment. By understanding potential risks and taking steps to mitigate them, they are able to invest with confidence and make decisions that lead to sustainable wealth growth.

Conclusion: A Strategic Approach to Investing

Smart investment strategies are essential for building sustainable wealth. By understanding the principles of asset allocation, real estate investing, portfolio diversification, and risk management, you can make informed decisions that align with your financial goals and risk tolerance. Whether you are just starting or looking to refine your investment approach, the key to success lies in developing a diversified portfolio and staying focused on long-term growth.

Investing isn't just about making money—it's about making money work for you. By employing smart strategies, you can ensure that your wealth continues to grow, providing you with the financial freedom to live life on your own terms.

In *The Unstoppable Road to Wealth Creation*, *The Things Wealthy People Do*, and *The Mind of a Trillionaire*, I've emphasized the importance of disciplined investing and the power of long-term wealth building. Now, it's time for you to take the next step in your financial journey by applying these principles to create your own sustainable wealth.

Chapter 11:

A Practical Guide to Financial Independence

Financial independence isn't a dream or a far-off goal—it's a process. It's the result of a series of smart decisions, disciplined actions, and a long-term vision for your life and wealth. It requires careful planning, wise investments, and a relentless commitment to creating a life where money works for you, not the other way around.

In *The Unstoppable Road to Wealth Creation*, I discussed how wealth building is not an overnight achievement but rather the result of consistent and deliberate actions over time. Similarly, in *The Things Wealthy People Do*, I explored the everyday habits of the wealthy, showing that financial independence is a culmination of both big moves and small, everyday financial decisions. In *The Mind of a Trillionaire*, we uncovered how the world's wealthiest individuals think about money and how they make it work for them.

Achieving financial independence isn't about getting rich quickly—it's about creating a sustainable, long-term plan that allows you to live life on your terms, without the constant stress of financial uncertainty. This chapter is a practical, actionable guide to help you design that life.

1. Define Your Vision of Financial Independence

Before you can achieve financial independence, you must first define what it looks like for you. Financial independence means different things to different people. For some, it's the ability to retire early. For others, it's the freedom to pursue passions without the constraints of a 9-to-5 job. In *The Unstoppable Road to Wealth Creation*, I highlighted the importance of creating a financial vision that aligns with your values and long-term goals.

The Power of Vision

Having a clear vision of your financial future serves as both your roadmap and your motivation. Vision provides clarity, helps you make decisions, and ensures that every action you take is aligned with your long-term goals. This is not just about accumulating wealth—it's about designing a life of financial freedom that enables you to focus on what truly matters.

Example: Imagine you define your financial independence as the ability to retire at 45 and live comfortably without the need to work. Your plan would involve setting specific financial goals, such as saving a set amount each month, investing wisely, and generating passive income streams that grow over time.

Actionable Tip:

Write down your vision for financial independence. Be as specific as possible. Do you want to travel? Start your own business? Spend more time with family? By visualizing your goals, you create a clear path to achieving them.

2. The Importance of Budgeting and Saving

One of the foundational principles of financial independence is living below your means. In *The Things Wealthy People Do*, I shared the financial habits of successful individuals, and one thing was clear: they all understood the importance of saving and budgeting. They knew that no matter how much money you make, it's how much you keep and invest that truly matters.

Saving Strategically

Saving is the first step toward financial independence. But it's not just about saving for the sake of it—it's about saving with a purpose. You must allocate your savings towards specific goals, whether it's building an emergency fund, saving for a down payment on a home, or investing in the stock market.

Example: Consider an individual who sets a goal to save 20% of their income each month. This might seem modest, but over time, this disciplined approach can create significant wealth, especially when compounded through smart investments.

Actionable Tip:

Track your expenses for a month. Identify areas where you can cut back on unnecessary spending and redirect that money toward savings or investments. Consider using a budgeting app to help you stay on track.

3. Developing Smart Investment Strategies

Investing is arguably the most effective way to build lasting wealth. In *The Unstoppable Road to Wealth Creation*, I emphasized the importance of starting early and making wise investment choices. Investing in stocks, real estate, bonds, and other assets can help you build the wealth needed to achieve financial independence.

The Power of Compounding

One of the most powerful concepts in investing is compound interest. In *The Mind of a Trillionaire*, we discussed how billionaires use compounding to grow their wealth. Even modest returns can lead to significant wealth over time when reinvested.

Example: Consider a person who starts investing $500 a month in a diversified stock portfolio with an average annual return of 8%. Over 30 years, their investment would grow significantly due to compounding, allowing them to achieve financial independence much sooner than they could have with just saving.

Actionable Tip:

Start investing today, even if it's a small amount. Look for investment vehicles that offer compound growth, such as stocks, mutual funds, and index funds. The earlier you start, the more you can take advantage of compounding.

4. Building Multiple Streams of Income

Financial independence is more achievable when you create multiple sources of income. Relying solely on a salary is risky because it ties you to one income stream. In *The Unstoppable Road to Wealth Creation*, we discussed how creating multiple income streams is essential to long-term wealth-building.

Types of Income Streams:

- **Active Income:** This is income you earn through your job or business. It's a direct exchange of your time and effort for money.

- **Passive Income:** This is income that comes from investments or assets that generate revenue with minimal effort, such as rental income, dividends from stocks, or royalties from intellectual property.

- **Side Hustles:** In addition to your primary income, side hustles, such as freelancing or launching a digital business, can provide additional revenue.

Example: An individual with a full-time job may also generate passive income by renting out a property or investing in dividend-paying stocks. This dual income stream allows them to build wealth without relying solely on their job.

Actionable Tip:

Identify opportunities for additional income streams. Look into investing in rental properties, starting an online business, or developing other passive income opportunities.

5. Managing Debt Wisely

Debt can be a major obstacle on the path to financial independence. In *The Things Wealthy People Do*, I explored how the wealthy manage debt—and often avoid unnecessary debt altogether. The key is to distinguish between good debt (debt used for investments that generate returns) and bad debt (debt used for consumption or non-productive purposes).

Getting Out of Debt

One of the first steps to achieving financial independence is paying off high-interest debt. This includes credit card debt, payday loans, and personal loans that carry high interest rates. By eliminating these debts, you free up more money to save and invest.

Example: An individual with credit card debt at 20% interest should prioritize paying off this debt before investing, as the interest costs are higher than the returns they could expect from most investments.

Actionable Tip:

Create a debt repayment plan. Focus on paying off high-interest debts first, then move to lower-interest debts. Once your debt is under control, you can direct more of your income toward saving and investing.

6. The Role of Entrepreneurship in Financial Independence

While investing and saving are critical, entrepreneurship can significantly accelerate your path to financial independence. In *The Unstoppable Road to Wealth Creation*, we discussed how many successful individuals created wealth by building businesses. Owning a business gives you control over your financial future and the potential for unlimited income.

Starting a Business

Starting a business can be daunting, but it's one of the most effective ways to gain financial independence. Whether it's a traditional business or an online venture, entrepreneurship offers the opportunity to create a scalable income stream.

Example: Consider an individual who starts an online business with low overhead costs. Over time, they scale the business by outsourcing tasks, automating processes, and growing their customer base. The business generates passive income, providing financial freedom.

Actionable Tip:

If entrepreneurship interests you, consider starting a side business while you're still employed. Use your spare time to research opportunities, build a business plan, and test the market. Once your business is profitable, you can transition to full-time entrepreneurship.

7. Protecting Your Wealth

Achieving financial independence is just the beginning. Protecting your wealth from unforeseen circumstances, such as economic downturns, lawsuits, or other financial risks, is just as important. In *The Mind of a Trillionaire*, I discussed how billionaires protect their wealth by diversifying, using insurance, and employing asset protection strategies.

Insurance and Asset Protection

Ensure that you have adequate insurance to protect your assets. This includes health insurance, life insurance, disability insurance, and property insurance. Additionally, consider setting up legal structures, such as trusts or limited liability companies (LLCs), to protect your wealth from legal claims.

Example: A business owner might set up an LLC to protect their personal assets from business liabilities. This structure ensures that if the business faces financial trouble, the owner's personal wealth remains intact.

Actionable Tip:

Review your insurance policies and legal protections. Consult with a financial advisor or attorney to ensure that your wealth is properly protected from risks.

Conclusion: Designing Your Path to Financial Independence

Achieving financial independence is a journey, not a destination. It requires vision, discipline, and smart decisions every step of the way. By following the principles outlined in this chapter—budgeting, saving, investing wisely, creating multiple income streams, managing debt, and protecting your wealth—you can take control of your financial future and create a life of independence and prosperity.

Remember, financial independence doesn't happen by accident. It's the result of deliberate action and strategic planning. So start today, set your goals, and begin building the foundation for the life you've always dreamed of.

Chapter 12:

The Discipline of Wealth Management

Achieving financial success is not solely about earning a high income; it's about managing and allocating that wealth effectively. Without discipline in wealth management, even the most lucrative earnings can dissipate over time. Wealthy individuals have a unique approach to managing their finances, focusing on long-term sustainability, strategic growth, and controlled spending. In *The Unstoppable Road to Wealth Creation*, we explored the importance of consistent effort, vision, and planning in building wealth. In *The Things Wealthy People Do*, we examined the daily habits of successful individuals, which emphasize financial discipline. Likewise, in *The Mind of a Trillionaire*, we uncovered how the wealthiest people think differently about money—viewing it not as a tool for immediate gratification but as a resource for building lasting, generational wealth.

In this chapter, we will explore the fundamental principles of wealth management. Whether you are just beginning your financial journey or are already on the road to prosperity, mastering wealth management can make the difference between accumulating wealth and losing it. The core components of wealth management include budgeting, controlling unnecessary spending, saving efficiently, and investing strategically. These skills form the backbone of any successful financial growth strategy.

1. The Importance of Financial Discipline

At the heart of wealth management lies one of the most critical elements: discipline. Financial discipline is the ability to make choices that align with long-term financial goals, even when faced with short-term temptations. It requires setting priorities, creating financial systems, and sticking to them. In *The Unstoppable Road to Wealth Creation*, I discussed how discipline is essential to wealth-building. It's not enough to simply make money; you must learn how to manage it effectively.

Defining Financial Discipline

Financial discipline involves more than just making a budget. It's about developing a mindset that places long-term wealth over immediate gratification. This means delaying consumption in favor of saving and investing for future growth. Wealthy individuals, particularly those in *The Mind of a Trillionaire*, practice this discipline consistently, viewing their wealth as a tool for creating more wealth.

Example: Take the case of an individual who earns a substantial salary but consistently overspends on luxury goods. While their income is high, their lack of financial discipline causes them to live paycheck to paycheck. On the other hand, someone with a similar income who adheres to disciplined financial practices, like budgeting and saving, can build lasting wealth over time.

Actionable Tip:

Develop a habit of saying "no" to unnecessary expenditures. Every time you resist an impulse purchase, you're building your financial discipline. Start small, and gradually increase your ability to make decisions that prioritize long-term financial health over short-term desires.

2. Mastering the Art of Budgeting

Budgeting is the cornerstone of wealth management. Without a clear understanding of where your money is going, it's impossible to manage your finances effectively. In *The Things Wealthy People Do*, we examined how successful individuals track their income and expenditures meticulously to ensure they stay on course with their financial goals. A solid budget allows you to allocate resources towards investments, savings, and necessary expenses, all while avoiding unnecessary debt.

The Power of Zero-Based Budgeting

One effective budgeting strategy that wealthy individuals often use is zero-based budgeting. In this approach, every dollar of your income is assigned a specific purpose—whether it's for bills, savings, or investments—until you've allocated all of it. The goal is to ensure that no money is left unaccounted for.

Example: Imagine you earn $5,000 per month. Instead of just setting aside a portion for savings and spending the rest, with zero-based budgeting, you assign specific amounts to various categories: $500 for savings, $300 for investments, $2,000 for living expenses, and so on. By the end of the process, every dollar has a purpose.

Actionable Tip:

Implement zero-based budgeting in your financial planning. For the next month, list all of your income and expenses, and ensure that every dollar is allocated to a specific purpose. This will help you avoid wasteful spending and stay focused on your financial goals.

3. Controlling Unnecessary Spending

One of the most significant barriers to wealth accumulation is unnecessary spending. Many people—whether they earn $30,000 or $300,000 a year—fall into the trap of spending money on non-essential items. Wealthy individuals understand that it's not about how much you make, but how much you keep. In *The Unstoppable Road to Wealth Creation*, I shared stories of individuals who mastered the art of controlling their spending to grow their wealth over time.

Identifying Non-Essential Expenses

The first step in controlling unnecessary spending is to identify where your money is going. Tracking every expense can be eye-opening. It's easy to overspend on small things—like dining out, subscription services, or impulse buys—that add up over time.

Example: Consider an individual who spends $100 a week on eating out. Over the course of a year, this amounts to $5,200. If that same money were invested instead, it could grow significantly, potentially compounding into a much larger sum over time.

Actionable Tip:

Audit your monthly spending. Identify areas where you can cut back, and redirect that money into savings or investments. Start by reducing discretionary spending—such as eating out or shopping—and reallocate those funds towards your financial growth.

4. Saving Efficiently

Saving money is a fundamental component of wealth management, but it's not just about putting money aside; it's about saving efficiently. In *The Unstoppable Road to Wealth Creation*, we explored how strategic saving—not just haphazardly putting money aside—can significantly impact your ability to build wealth. Wealthy individuals understand the importance of allocating savings to specific goals, such as an emergency fund, retirement savings, or investment opportunities.

Creating Savings Goals

A key part of efficient saving is setting clear, achievable goals. These goals should align with your long-term financial vision and be broken down into manageable steps. The more specific you are with your goals, the easier it will be to stay on track.

Example: You may set a goal to save $20,000 for a down payment on a house in three years. To achieve this, you need to save about $555 per month. By breaking down the goal into smaller chunks, you can track your progress and stay motivated.

Actionable Tip:

Set specific savings goals for both the short term (e.g., building an emergency fund) and long term (e.g., retirement savings). Automate your savings whenever possible to ensure you're consistently contributing toward your goals.

5. The Power of Investment in Wealth Management

While saving is important, investing is where wealth can truly grow. In *The Mind of a Trillionaire*, we discussed how billionaires approach investing—not just for immediate returns but for long-term wealth preservation and growth. Wealthy individuals tend to diversify their investments across various asset classes to reduce risk and ensure steady growth. They understand that investing isn't a one-time event but an ongoing strategy.

Types of Investments for Wealth Growth

There are several types of investments to consider, including:

- **Stocks and Bonds:** These are common investment vehicles for individuals looking to build wealth over time.

- **Real Estate:** Many wealthy individuals accumulate wealth through property investments, which provide both passive income and long-term appreciation.

- **Alternative Investments:** These can include private equity, venture capital, and commodities—investment types that wealthy individuals often use to diversify their portfolios.

Example: Consider an individual who invests in a diversified portfolio of stocks, bonds, and real estate. Over time, the growth from these assets allows them to achieve financial independence and build generational wealth.

Actionable Tip:

Start investing as soon as possible, even if it's a small amount. Educate yourself on different investment vehicles and build a diversified portfolio. Over time, your investments will compound, helping you grow your wealth efficiently.

6. Understanding the Role of Taxes in Wealth Management

One often overlooked aspect of wealth management is understanding the role of taxes. In *The Unstoppable Road to Wealth Creation*, I emphasized how taxes can erode wealth if not properly managed. Wealthy individuals take great care to minimize their tax liabilities by leveraging tax-efficient investment strategies, utilizing tax-advantaged accounts, and working with financial advisors to implement tax-saving strategies.

Tax Strategies for Wealth Preservation

Some common tax strategies include:

- **Maximizing Contributions to Tax-Advantaged Accounts:** Contributing to accounts like IRAs, 401(k)s, or HSAs can reduce your taxable income and help you save for retirement.
- **Tax-Loss Harvesting:** This strategy involves selling investments that are underperforming to offset capital gains taxes.

Example: A person contributing to a 401(k) not only saves for retirement but also reduces their taxable income for the year, leading to potential tax savings.

Actionable Tip:

Consult a tax professional to help you optimize your tax strategy. Take advantage of tax-advantaged accounts and tax-efficient investment strategies to minimize the impact of taxes on your wealth.

7. Continuous Learning and Adaptation

Wealth management is not a one-time endeavor; it's a lifelong process of learning and adaptation. As your financial situation evolves, so too should your strategies for managing wealth. In *The Mind of a Trillionaire*, we discussed how the world's wealthiest individuals continually learn and adapt their financial strategies to changing circumstances.

Staying Educated About Financial Management

Wealthy individuals understand the importance of staying informed about economic trends, market shifts, and new financial strategies. By constantly educating yourself, you can ensure that your wealth management strategies remain relevant and effective.

Example: An individual who stays informed about market trends can make informed investment decisions and adapt their financial strategies to maximize growth opportunities.

Actionable Tip:

Commit to continuous financial education. Read books, attend seminars, and seek advice from financial experts to keep your knowledge up to date.

Conclusion

Mastering wealth management is an ongoing process that requires discipline, planning, and strategic thinking. It's not about making a lot of money—it's about managing that money in a way that allows it to grow and work for you. By budgeting wisely, controlling unnecessary spending, saving efficiently, and making informed investment decisions, you can build a solid foundation for lasting wealth.

Remember, financial discipline is a mindset that empowers you to make decisions aligned with your long-term goals. Stay focused, stay disciplined, and watch your wealth grow.

Chapter 13:

Harnessing Technology for Financial Advancement

The world of wealth creation has undergone a profound transformation in recent years, largely due to the rapid advancement of technology. From digital investment platforms to apps that automate savings, technology has become an integral tool in the wealth-building process. In this chapter, we will explore how you can harness the power of technology to enhance income generation, optimize wealth management, and streamline your financial growth. Technology provides access to new investment opportunities, makes wealth management more efficient, and offers tools to scale businesses in ways that were once unimaginable.

In *The Unstoppable Road to Wealth Creation*, we emphasized that creating and sustaining wealth requires leveraging the tools available to you. Similarly, *The Things Wealthy People Do* highlighted how successful individuals utilize available resources to maximize their financial potential. In *The Mind of a Trillionaire*, we explored how technology plays a significant role in the thinking and strategies of the world's wealthiest individuals. This chapter continues the conversation by offering actionable insights into how technology can be a game-changer in your wealth-building journey.

1. Digital Platforms for Investment

One of the most significant ways technology has impacted wealth creation is through digital investment platforms. These platforms provide unprecedented access to investment opportunities, from stocks and bonds to real estate and cryptocurrency. Gone are the days when investing was only for the wealthy or those with insider knowledge. Today, anyone with an internet connection can invest in a variety of assets with just a few clicks.

Investment Apps and Online Brokerage Platforms

Apps such as Robinhood, E*TRADE, and TD Ameritrade have revolutionized stock investing by making it easy to buy, sell, and trade securities without the need for a traditional broker. These platforms provide access to real-time market data, allowing users to make informed decisions and execute trades quickly. Additionally, many of these platforms offer low or no commission fees, which means you can invest without incurring significant costs that might erode your returns.

In *The Unstoppable Road to Wealth Creation*, I discussed the importance of investing early and taking advantage of compound interest. With digital platforms, this has never been easier. Even small amounts of money can be invested regularly, resulting in significant wealth accumulation over time.

Example:

Consider an individual who begins investing $50 per week into an index fund using an app like Robinhood. Over time, with regular contributions and the magic of compounding, their investment grows. By focusing on long-term gains rather than short-term fluctuations, they're able to build wealth steadily. This concept is central to the wealth-building strategies mentioned in *The Mind of a Trillionaire*—investing with a long-term vision.

Robo-Advisors and Automated Investing

Robo-advisors such as Betterment and Wealthfront take the guesswork out of investing by providing automated portfolio management services. These platforms use algorithms to build and manage a diversified portfolio based on your risk tolerance, investment goals, and time horizon. In essence, robo-advisors offer a low-cost, hands-off approach to investing, making them ideal for those new to wealth management or anyone who prefers to delegate their investment decisions to technology.

Actionable   **Tip:**

If you're looking to simplify your investment strategy, consider using a robo-advisor. They are excellent for beginners and those looking for a passive investment strategy that still delivers long-term growth.

2. Automating Savings for Consistent Growth

Automation is another technology-driven strategy that can have a significant impact on your wealth-building journey. In *The Things Wealthy People Do*, we saw that consistent saving and investing were essential habits of the financially successful. Automation takes the effort out of saving and ensures that you're consistently contributing toward your financial goals.

Automated Savings Apps

Apps such as Acorns and Digit automatically transfer small amounts of money from your checking account into savings or investment accounts. These apps use algorithms to round up purchases to the nearest dollar and invest or save the difference. This process allows you to save and invest without even thinking about it.

Example:

If you purchase a coffee for $2.75, the app will round the charge up to $3 and invest or save the extra $0.25. These small contributions add up over time, helping you accumulate wealth effortlessly.

In *The Unstoppable Road to Wealth Creation*, I discussed the importance of starting small and remaining consistent. Automated savings apps make this process seamless, allowing you to accumulate wealth without having to consciously set aside money each month. By automating your savings, you remove the temptation to spend and ensure that your money is working for you.

Actionable Tip:

Download a savings app and set it up to round up your purchases or automatically transfer a small percentage of your income into a savings or investment account. This allows you to save without any effort on your part, making it easier to grow your wealth over time.

3. Using Technology to Scale Your Business

As an entrepreneur, technology offers many ways to scale your business and reach a wider audience. In *The Mind of a Trillionaire*, we explored how successful business leaders use technology to expand their reach, improve customer experiences, and optimize business processes. Whether you run a brick-and-mortar store, an online business, or a hybrid model, there are digital tools that can help you grow and manage your business more efficiently.

E-Commerce Platforms and Online Marketplaces

Platforms such as Shopify, Amazon, and Etsy allow entrepreneurs to set up online stores and reach customers worldwide. These platforms handle everything from payment processing to inventory management, allowing you to focus on growing your business. In *The Unstoppable Road to Wealth Creation*, we saw that businesses that embrace digital tools are able to scale more rapidly and reach larger audiences.

For example, JAY T CLOTHING, your clothing brand, leverages online platforms to sell custom-made clothing across various online merchants and marketplaces, including Amazon, eBay, Shopify, and Facebook Marketplace. These platforms help streamline sales, manage inventory, and drive revenue—all while giving you the ability to reach a global market.

Actionable Tip:

If you haven't already, set up an online store or leverage existing platforms like Amazon or Shopify to sell your products or services. Embrace the power of e-commerce to expand your reach and grow your business.

Digital Marketing Tools

Marketing your business digitally can accelerate growth in ways that traditional methods can't. Tools like Google Ads, Facebook Ads, and Instagram Ads allow you to reach a global audience, target specific demographics, and track the performance of your ads in real-time. Social media platforms like TikTok, Instagram, and YouTube have become essential tools for brand-building and engaging with customers.

In *The Things Wealthy People Do*, we discussed the importance of branding and marketing. Wealthy individuals understand that branding isn't just about visibility; it's about building trust and creating a lasting connection with customers. Using social media and digital marketing tools is key to this process.

Example:

A small business owner can use Instagram to showcase their products, create engaging content, and interact with followers. By targeting the right audience and using ads effectively, they can build a loyal customer base and generate substantial revenue.

Actionable Tip:

Utilize social media platforms and digital advertising tools to promote your business. Experiment with different types of content—such as videos, blogs, and infographics—and track the results to refine your marketing strategy.

4. Blockchain and Cryptocurrency as Emerging Investment Vehicles

The rise of blockchain technology and cryptocurrencies has introduced new and innovative ways to invest and build wealth. While cryptocurrency remains volatile, it offers a new avenue for diversification in your investment portfolio. Blockchain technology, which underpins cryptocurrencies like Bitcoin and Ethereum, has broader applications in various industries, including finance, healthcare, and logistics.

In *The Mind of a Trillionaire,* we touched on how the wealthiest individuals view emerging technologies as opportunities for diversification and growth. They recognize that being early adopters of new technologies can provide significant financial returns.

Investing in Cryptocurrency

Cryptocurrency offers the potential for substantial returns, although it comes with higher risk. Platforms such as Coinbase and Binance make it easy to buy, sell, and trade cryptocurrencies. For those willing to take the risk, cryptocurrency can be an exciting addition to a diversified investment portfolio.

Example:

An individual who invested $1,000 in Bitcoin in 2015 would have seen that investment grow exponentially as the price of Bitcoin soared in the following years. While the market is volatile, strategic investing in cryptocurrency can yield massive returns.

Actionable Tip:

If you're interested in cryptocurrency, start small and use reputable platforms to buy and trade digital currencies. Diversify your portfolio to manage risk, and stay informed about developments in blockchain and cryptocurrency technologies.

5. Financial Apps for Budgeting and Tracking

Another way technology can help you manage your wealth is through budgeting and expense tracking apps. Tools like Mint, YNAB (You Need A Budget), and PocketGuard help you track your spending, set budgets, and monitor your progress toward financial goals. These apps automatically categorize your transactions, making it easy to see where your money is going.

Example:

A person using Mint might discover that they're spending more on subscriptions than they realized. By using this information, they can cancel unnecessary services and redirect that money into savings or investments.

Actionable Tip:

Download a budgeting or tracking app to gain insight into your spending habits. Use the data provided to optimize your finances, cut unnecessary expenses, and allocate more money toward your wealth-building goals.

Conclusion

Technology is a powerful ally in your wealth-building journey. From digital investment platforms to automated savings apps, there are countless tools available to help you make, manage, and grow your wealth. As highlighted in *The Unstoppable Road to Wealth Creation*, wealth isn't just about hard work; it's also about working smart. Embracing technology allows you to do just that—automating tedious tasks, accessing new opportunities, and optimizing your financial strategies.

As we've seen throughout this chapter, technology can accelerate your journey to financial success, but it's crucial to approach it strategically. Whether you're investing, saving, or scaling your business, the key is consistency and informed decision-making. By incorporating the right digital tools into your wealth-building strategy, you can maximize your potential for financial growth and achieve the success you've always dreamed of.

The opportunities are endless for those who are willing to embrace technology. The question is, are you ready to harness its power?

Chapter 14:

Risk, Reward, and Wealth Creation

Wealth creation is not for the faint of heart. It requires courage, persistence, and the ability to embrace risk. However, contrary to popular belief, the wealthiest individuals are not risk-takers in the sense of reckless gamblers. Instead, they are calculated risk-takers. They understand the relationship between risk and reward and know that without taking risks, significant financial growth is impossible. In this chapter, we explore how understanding and managing risk can unlock new opportunities for financial advancement and long-term wealth creation.

The Fundamental Relationship Between Risk and Reward

At its core, the concept of risk and reward is simple: the higher the potential return, the higher the associated risk. Risk is an inherent part of any venture that aims for financial growth. Whether you're investing in the stock market, starting a business, or making a real estate acquisition, there is no guarantee of success. However, without taking some form of calculated risk, the opportunity for reward remains limited.

In *The Unstoppable Road to Wealth Creation*, we discussed how taking small, smart risks over time can compound into substantial wealth. In *The Things Wealthy People Do*, we learned that wealthy individuals understand that calculated risks are the stepping stones to achieving extraordinary results. And in *The Mind of a Trillionaire*, we explored how the world's wealthiest people approach risk with discipline and strategy—leveraging it as a tool to unlock new financial possibilities.

The key takeaway is that risk is unavoidable. The question is not whether or not to take risks but how to take them strategically. Wealth is built by those who understand the dynamics of risk, make informed decisions, and take action without letting fear hold them back.

Understanding Different Types of Risk

Before diving into strategies for managing risk, it's important to understand the various types of risk that can impact wealth creation.

1. Market Risk

Market risk refers to the risk that an investment's value will decrease due to factors such as economic downturns, political instability, or market volatility. For example, when the stock market crashes, the value of stocks across the board can significantly drop. This risk is often associated with the purchase of stocks, bonds, or other market-dependent assets.

In *The Unstoppable Road to Wealth Creation*, I highlighted how diversification across different asset classes—such as stocks, bonds, and real estate—can help mitigate market risk. By spreading investments across multiple markets, you protect yourself from the impact of market downturns in any one sector.

Example:

Consider an investor who has all their savings tied up in tech stocks. If the technology sector takes a hit due to regulatory changes or market corrections, their entire portfolio could suffer. A more diversified portfolio—including investments in real estate, bonds, and international stocks—can help cushion the blow during such downturns.

2. Business Risk

Business risk involves the uncertainty and challenges faced by businesses in their operations. Factors such as competition, customer preferences, operational inefficiencies, or failure to innovate can negatively impact a company's profitability. When building wealth through entrepreneurship, understanding business risks is essential.

In *The Things Wealthy People Do*, we saw that successful business owners understand the risks involved in scaling their companies. They make strategic decisions that minimize these risks while simultaneously positioning themselves for growth. These decisions may include choosing the right partners, maintaining efficient operations, or managing cash flow carefully.

Example:

Consider a startup company in the tech industry that has developed a new product. The company faces several risks, including product failure, market rejection, and the challenge of securing funding. Despite these risks, the company can reduce the likelihood of failure by conducting thorough market research, seeking investor backing, and constantly innovating to stay ahead of competitors.

3. Investment Risk

Investment risk is the risk of losing capital or failing to achieve the desired returns from an investment. This type of risk varies depending on the type of investment vehicle you choose. For example, stocks carry more risk than bonds, while real estate tends to have lower risk but requires significant capital upfront.

As discussed in *The Mind of a Trillionaire*, the wealthiest individuals manage investment risk by diversifying their portfolios, maintaining liquidity, and leveraging advanced financial strategies such as hedging and options trading.

Example:
A person investing in real estate may face risk in the form of property depreciation, difficulty finding tenants, or rising interest rates. However, this risk can be mitigated through careful research, location selection, and risk management strategies like insurance or property upgrades.

4. Credit Risk

Credit risk arises when lending money to individuals or businesses. This risk occurs when the borrower defaults on repayment, potentially leading to financial loss. Credit risk is a concern when investing in bonds, lending to others, or engaging in any form of financing.

To minimize credit risk, it's important to assess the creditworthiness of the borrower and ensure that terms are favorable and secure. This concept was explored in *The Unstoppable Road to Wealth Creation*, where I stressed the importance of making informed lending decisions and using secure collateral when lending money.

Calculating and Managing Risk

Now that we understand the types of risk involved in wealth creation, the next step is learning how to calculate and manage these risks.

1. Risk Tolerance and Financial Goals

Understanding your risk tolerance is essential to making smart, calculated decisions. Risk tolerance refers to your willingness and ability to endure financial losses in the pursuit of higher returns. It's a personal decision based on factors such as your age, financial goals, income stability, and time horizon.

In *The Unstoppable Road to Wealth Creation*, I advised readers to assess their risk tolerance before making major financial decisions. A person in their 20s may have a higher risk tolerance because they have time to recover from losses, while someone nearing retirement may prefer more conservative investments with lower risks.

Example:

If you're building wealth over the long term, you might be more inclined to invest in high-growth stocks or real estate development projects, which carry higher risks but can yield substantial returns. However, if you're nearing retirement, you may prefer fixed-income investments such as bonds, which offer more stability but lower returns.

2. Diversification

Diversification is one of the most effective strategies for managing risk. By spreading your investments across different asset classes, industries, and geographic regions, you reduce the likelihood that a single poor-performing investment will wipe out your entire portfolio.

In *The Mind of a Trillionaire*, we saw how the world's wealthiest individuals use diversification not only to protect themselves from risks but also to position themselves for growth across various sectors. Diversification helps create a balanced portfolio that can weather different economic conditions.

Example:

Consider someone with a portfolio made up of 60% stocks, 30% real estate, and 10% cash. If the stock market crashes, their real estate investments may still perform well, keeping their overall wealth intact. In contrast, someone with a portfolio entirely made up of stocks would face a more significant loss.

3. Insurance as a Risk Mitigation Tool

Insurance is a critical tool for managing financial risk, especially when it comes to protecting your assets. Whether you're insuring a property, your business, or your life, having the right type of insurance ensures that you're covered in case of unexpected events that could derail your wealth-building plans.

In *The Things Wealthy People Do*, we discussed how the wealthy use insurance to protect their assets and investments. This might include life insurance, business insurance, or property insurance. By ensuring their assets are protected, they can take on more risk in other areas of their portfolio without exposing themselves to undue financial harm.

Example:

If you're a business owner, taking out liability insurance ensures that your business is protected from legal claims. This allows you to take more calculated risks, knowing that you're protected in the event of an unforeseen setback.

4. Hedging and Risk Management Strategies

Hedging is a strategy used by investors to offset potential losses in one investment by taking an opposite position in another. This can be done through the use of derivatives, such as options or futures contracts, which allow you to lock in profits or limit losses.

In *The Mind of a Trillionaire*, we explored how the wealthiest individuals use sophisticated financial tools, such as hedging, to manage risk and ensure that their investments continue to grow despite market fluctuations.

Example:

A hedge fund manager might use options to protect their investment in a stock. If they own shares in a company, they may purchase a put option that gives them the right to sell the stock at a predetermined price. This way, if the stock's value declines, they can limit their losses.

Conclusion: Embracing Risk for Wealth Creation

In the pursuit of wealth, risk is inevitable. However, by understanding the relationship between risk and reward, assessing your risk tolerance, and utilizing strategies like diversification, insurance, and hedging, you can manage and mitigate risk in ways that maximize your potential for growth.

As discussed in *The Unstoppable Road to Wealth Creation*, building wealth requires a mindset that embraces calculated risks. It's not about avoiding risk entirely, but about making informed decisions that allow you to take strategic risks that can propel you toward your financial goals.

The wealthiest individuals understand that without taking risks, significant rewards are not possible. They are not reckless gamblers, but rather intelligent decision-makers who leverage calculated risk as a tool for financial advancement. By adopting a similar mindset and approach to risk, you can unlock new opportunities and build sustainable wealth over the long term.

As you embark on your wealth-building journey, remember that risk is not your enemy—it's an essential part of the process. With the right strategies and a clear understanding of how to manage risk, you can create lasting financial success.

Section 3:

Sustaining and Expanding Financial Influence (Legacy & Long-Term Impact)

Chapter 15:

Protecting and Preserving Wealth

Accumulating wealth is a significant achievement, but it is only half of the financial journey. The true test of financial success is not just in how much wealth you amass, but in how well you protect and preserve that wealth for the long term. In this chapter, we will explore strategies and tools to safeguard your financial assets from risks such as inflation, taxes, market fluctuations, and unforeseen circumstances. We'll also discuss the importance of building a legacy, ensuring that your wealth continues to grow, and remains secure for future generations.

The Importance of Protecting Wealth

In *The Unstoppable Road to Wealth Creation*, we learned that wealth creation is a continuous process of reinvesting, optimizing opportunities, and making informed decisions. However, as you begin to build your wealth, the next logical step is to protect it. Protection ensures that your hard-earned assets are not easily eroded by inflation, taxes, or unexpected life events, such as illness or economic downturns.

Wealth preservation is about being proactive and creating a plan that not only safeguards your wealth but also allows it to continue to grow over time. For the wealthiest individuals, protecting their assets is not a passive act. It requires intentional strategies, including legal protections, insurance, and tax-efficient planning.

Strategies for Protecting and Preserving Wealth

1. Asset Allocation and Diversification

One of the primary strategies for protecting wealth is proper asset allocation. In *The Things Wealthy People Do*, we saw how wealthy individuals diversify their portfolios to minimize risk and protect their wealth from volatility in any one market. The concept of diversification involves spreading your investments across various asset classes, industries, and geographical regions to ensure that your wealth is not too heavily exposed to the fluctuations of any single investment.

For example, if the stock market is experiencing a downturn, your investments in real estate, bonds, or international stocks might still perform well, thus protecting your overall portfolio from loss. In *The Mind of a Trillionaire*, we saw how billionaires use diversification not just across different asset classes but also across industries, ensuring that their portfolios are resilient to market fluctuations.

Example:
Consider someone with a portfolio made up of 60% stocks, 30% real estate, and 10% cash. If the stock market crashes, their real estate

investments may still perform well, maintaining overall wealth. In contrast, someone with a portfolio entirely made up of stocks would face a more significant loss. Wealth preservation through asset allocation ensures that the risks of one investment are mitigated by others.

2. Inflation Protection

Inflation is one of the most significant threats to wealth preservation. Over time, the purchasing power of money decreases due to inflation, which erodes the real value of your wealth. As we explored in *The Unstoppable Road to Wealth Creation*, inflation can quickly diminish the value of cash holdings and other low-yielding assets. To preserve wealth in the face of inflation, it's essential to invest in assets that tend to outpace inflation.

Real estate has long been a favored asset for wealth preservation because it tends to appreciate over time, outpacing inflation. Similarly, **gold** and other precious metals have historically been seen as safe havens against inflation.

Example:

Let's say you have $1 million in cash, but inflation is running at 3% annually. After one year, your $1 million would be worth $970,000 in today's dollars. However, if you had invested that $1 million in real estate or a diversified portfolio of stocks and bonds, the value of your assets would likely have outpaced inflation, ensuring that your wealth remained intact.

In *The Things Wealthy People Do*, we discussed how wealthy individuals use inflation-hedging investments, such as real estate and precious metals, to preserve their wealth. These assets not only grow over time but also provide a hedge against the erosion of purchasing power.

3. Tax Planning and Efficiency

Taxes are one of the biggest drains on wealth if not managed properly. Taxation can significantly reduce the growth of your wealth, especially if you are not taking advantage of tax-efficient strategies. In *The Mind of a Trillionaire*, we explored how the wealthiest individuals use tax strategies to minimize their tax liabilities. These strategies include investing in tax-advantaged accounts, using trusts, and structuring businesses in a way that minimizes taxes.

For example, investing in tax-deferred accounts like 401(k)s or IRAs allows you to grow your wealth without paying taxes on the gains until you withdraw the funds, typically in retirement when you may be in a lower tax bracket. In addition, creating a **trust** can help shield your wealth from estate taxes and ensure that your assets are passed on to future generations without excessive tax burdens.

Example:

Consider a high-net-worth individual who invests $100,000 in a tax-advantaged retirement account. The investment grows for several years without being taxed. If they had invested that same amount in a taxable account, they would have had to pay capital gains taxes on the appreciation each year, which would have reduced the overall growth of the investment.

4. Insurance as a Protective Tool

Insurance is another essential component of wealth preservation. Whether it's life insurance, property insurance, liability insurance, or health insurance, having the right coverage protects you from unforeseen events that could otherwise threaten your wealth. In *The Unstoppable Road to Wealth Creation*, I highlighted how wealthy individuals use insurance to safeguard their assets and mitigate financial risks.

Life insurance, for instance, ensures that your family is financially secure in the event of your death. **Disability insurance** protects your income in case you become unable to work due to illness or injury. **Property insurance** protects valuable assets such as real estate, cars, or business property from damage or theft.

Example:

If you own multiple properties, having adequate property insurance ensures that in the event of a fire, flood, or other damage, your assets are protected, and you are not left with a massive financial burden. Similarly, if you have a successful business, liability insurance can protect you from legal claims that could jeopardize your wealth.

5. Estate Planning and Wealth Transfer

Preserving wealth also involves planning for the transfer of assets to future generations. **Estate planning** ensures that your wealth is passed on according to your wishes and with minimal tax implications. In *The Things Wealthy People Do*, we discussed how the wealthy often create comprehensive estate plans that include **wills**, **trusts**, and **advanced**

directives to preserve their wealth and provide for their heirs.

One of the most significant benefits of estate planning is its ability to minimize **estate taxes**, which can take a substantial portion of your wealth when it's passed on to your heirs. Using strategies like **generation-skipping trusts** or **family limited partnerships** can help reduce estate taxes while also providing for future generations.

Example:

Imagine a family-owned business that has been passed down for generations. Without proper estate planning, the heirs could be faced with high estate taxes that could force them to sell the business. However, by setting up a family trust and structuring the transfer of assets in a tax-efficient manner, the family can preserve the business for future generations and ensure that it continues to thrive.

6. Building a Legacy

In *The Mind of a Trillionaire*, we explored the concept of legacy, which is a vital part of wealth preservation. The wealthiest individuals are not just concerned with protecting their own wealth; they are also focused on creating a lasting legacy that will benefit future generations. This includes not only financial wealth but also values, knowledge, and family traditions that can be passed down.

To build a lasting legacy, it's important to instill financial literacy and responsibility in the next generation. This might involve setting up educational funds for your children or grandchildren, teaching them about wealth management, and ensuring they understand the importance of preserving and growing the family's wealth.

Example:

A family patriarch might establish a foundation that provides scholarships for future generations, ensuring that the family's legacy of education continues. Alternatively, a successful entrepreneur may create a family office to manage the family's wealth and ensure it continues to grow across generations.

Conclusion: Ensuring Wealth for Future Generations

The ability to protect and preserve wealth is crucial to ensuring long-term financial security. As we explored in *The Unstoppable Road to Wealth Creation*, wealth creation is only part of the journey. Protecting and preserving your wealth allows you to enjoy the fruits of your labor while also safeguarding your assets for future generations.

Through strategic asset allocation, inflation protection, tax planning, insurance, estate planning, and building a legacy, you can ensure that your wealth remains secure and continues to grow over time. Wealth preservation requires proactive, strategic decisions, but by taking these steps, you can protect your financial future and leave a lasting legacy that benefits those who come after you.

The wealthiest individuals understand that wealth is not just about accumulation—it's about preservation. With the right strategies in place, you can protect your assets from inflation, taxes, and unforeseen circumstances, ensuring that your wealth remains strong and secure for generations to come.

Chapter 16:

Building a Legacy of Generational Wealth

In today's fast-paced world, financial success is often seen as a personal achievement—a way to live a comfortable, secure life for yourself and your loved ones. However, true wealth is not just about enjoying the fruits of your labor in the present; it's about building a legacy that transcends generations. A legacy of generational wealth is one that ensures your descendants will continue to thrive long after you've passed, while also preserving the values, traditions, and principles that you hold dear. In this chapter, we will explore how to build such a legacy—one that stands the test of time and provides a foundation for your family's future success.

The Importance of Building Generational Wealth

As we discussed in *The Unstoppable Road to Wealth Creation*, creating wealth is a journey that requires consistent effort, smart decision-making, and the ability to seize opportunities. But wealth is not only about personal satisfaction; it's about creating something that benefits future generations. The wealthiest individuals don't focus only on their own financial security—they plan for the future, ensuring that their legacy lives on.

Generational wealth is wealth that is passed down from one generation to the next. Unlike the fleeting nature of personal wealth, which can be squandered in a single generation, generational wealth is designed to grow and compound over time. It's the result of thoughtful estate planning, disciplined investing, and making decisions that align with long-term goals rather than short-term gratification.

How to Build a Legacy of Generational Wealth

1. Strategic Estate Planning

One of the cornerstones of building a generational wealth legacy is **estate planning**. In *The Things Wealthy People Do*, we discussed how the wealthiest individuals are intentional about how their wealth is distributed after their passing. Estate planning ensures that your wealth is transferred to your heirs efficiently, while minimizing taxes and avoiding legal complexities.

Wills and Trusts:

A **will** outlines how you want your assets distributed after your death. However, a will only goes into effect after probate, a process that can be lengthy and costly. On the other hand, a **trust** is a legal entity that can hold assets for your heirs. Trusts can be set up to distribute assets according to your wishes, often avoiding the need for probate and offering more flexibility.

In *The Mind of a Trillionaire*, we explored how billionaires use trusts to not only pass on their wealth but also protect it from taxes and creditors. A trust allows you to control when and how your heirs receive their inheritance. You can also set specific terms, such as ensuring that your children receive their inheritance only after they reach a certain age or complete a certain educational level.

Example:

Imagine a successful entrepreneur who has built a multi-million-dollar company. Rather than leaving all of their assets in a will, they set up a **family trust** that ensures their children and grandchildren receive regular distributions from the trust while still allowing the wealth to grow. By doing so, they avoid the delays and expenses of probate, and their wealth continues to benefit future generations.

2. Creating Trusts and Foundations

Another effective way to build a legacy is through the establishment of **trusts** and **foundations**. In *The Unstoppable Road to Wealth Creation*, we discussed the importance of creating structures that provide long-term benefits and preserve wealth. Trusts can be used to protect assets, reduce taxes, and provide for the ongoing needs of your family.

A **family foundation** is another powerful tool that allows you to not only preserve wealth but also instill your values into future generations. A foundation can be established to support charitable causes, fund education, or promote your family's legacy of entrepreneurship. In *The Mind of a Trillionaire*, we highlighted how some of the world's wealthiest families have used foundations to create a lasting impact, both financially and socially.

Example:

Consider the Walton family, who created the **Walton Family Foundation**, which supports educational initiatives, community development, and economic empowerment. By establishing a foundation, the Walton family has ensured that their wealth continues to support the values they hold dear, while also providing for the future needs of their descendants.

3. Smart Investment Choices for Long-Term Growth

Investing is a critical part of building a legacy of generational wealth. In *The Things Wealthy People Do*, we learned that wealthy individuals make smart investment choices that not only provide short-term returns but also ensure long-term growth. By building a diversified portfolio, including **stocks, real estate, bonds**, and **business ventures**, you can ensure that your wealth continues to grow, providing for future generations.

Real Estate:

Real estate has long been a cornerstone of wealth-building and wealth preservation. In *The Unstoppable Road to Wealth Creation*, we discussed how real estate investment offers numerous opportunities to build wealth through appreciation, rental income, and tax benefits. Real estate investments tend to grow in value over time, making them ideal for passing down to future generations.

Stocks and Bonds:

Equity investments, such as **stocks**, and fixed-income investments, such as **bonds**, are essential parts of a diversified portfolio. These investments offer both growth potential and stability. In *The Mind of a Trillionaire*, we explored how billionaires invest not only for today but for the future, ensuring that their wealth is secure and growing for generations.

Business Ownership:

Owning a family business is another way to create generational wealth. By building a company that can be passed down to future generations, you provide not only financial security but also opportunities for future generations to thrive. In *The Things Wealthy People Do*, we discussed how successful entrepreneurs create businesses that provide long-term financial benefits and serve as a legacy.

Example:

Consider a family-owned real estate investment firm that has been passed down for multiple generations. The business continues to generate revenue and grow in value, allowing each generation to expand their portfolio and create new opportunities. The family has not only preserved their wealth but has also created a thriving business that supports future generations.

4. Building a Strong Financial Education Foundation

Wealth is not simply about accumulating assets—it's about passing on the knowledge to manage and grow those assets. In *The Unstoppable Road to*

Wealth Creation, we discussed the importance of financial literacy. One of the keys to building generational wealth is ensuring that each successive generation understands how to manage money, make smart financial decisions, and preserve wealth.

Financial   Literacy:

Start teaching your children and grandchildren about money early. Teach them the importance of saving, investing, and managing debt. By instilling financial education at a young age, you ensure that the next generation is prepared to handle the wealth you leave them.

Example:

Imagine a family who sets up a series of **financial education workshops** for their children and grandchildren. These workshops teach them about budgeting, investing, and financial independence. As the next generation grows, they not only inherit wealth but also the knowledge needed to preserve and grow that wealth.

5. Philanthropy as Part of Your Legacy

Philanthropy plays a significant role in building a legacy that transcends financial wealth. In *The Mind of a Trillionaire*, we saw how the wealthiest individuals use their fortunes to make a difference in the world, whether through charitable giving, creating scholarships, or supporting causes that are important to them. By giving back, you not only leave a lasting impact on the world, but you also set an example for future generations.

Example:

Consider the Bill and Melinda Gates Foundation, which has become one of the largest charitable organizations in the world. Through their philanthropy, the Gates family has not only made a significant impact on global health and education but has also ensured that their wealth continues to benefit society for generations to come.

6. Wealth Preservation Through Tax Planning

In order to preserve wealth for future generations, it's essential to be mindful of taxes. As we discussed in *The Unstoppable Road to Wealth Creation*, taxes can take a significant chunk out of your wealth. Strategic tax planning ensures that your assets are transferred in the most tax-efficient manner possible.

Tax-Efficient Transfers:

Setting up trusts, foundations, and charitable donations can help reduce the tax burden on your estate. Additionally, utilizing tax-deferred or tax-exempt investment vehicles, such as IRAs or 529 education savings plans, can ensure that your wealth continues to grow without the drag of high taxes.

Example:

A family that has successfully managed its wealth might set up a **dynasty trust**, which allows wealth to be passed down through multiple generations without being subject to estate taxes. By doing so, they protect their wealth from excessive taxation and ensure that their heirs will benefit from it for years to come.

Conclusion: Leaving a Lasting Legacy

Building a legacy of generational wealth requires careful planning, strategic investments, and a commitment to ensuring that your wealth continues to grow and benefit future generations. By focusing on strategic estate planning, creating trusts and foundations, making smart investment choices, building financial literacy, engaging in philanthropy, and preserving wealth through tax planning, you can ensure that your wealth continues to thrive long after you're gone.

In *The Unstoppable Road to Wealth Creation*, we discussed the importance of a growth mindset and building wealth that lasts. This is the foundation upon which generational wealth is built. By focusing on long-term strategies and making decisions that benefit future generations, you can create a legacy that not only provides for your family's financial future but also instills values that transcend wealth itself.

Building generational wealth is not just about accumulating assets—it's about creating a legacy of financial security, opportunity, and impact that will benefit your descendants for years to come. By taking intentional steps today, you can ensure that your wealth continues to grow and that your legacy lives on.

Chapter 17:

Giving with Purpose

Wealth isn't solely meant to improve the quality of life for the individual who has accumulated it. True wealth is defined by its potential to make a lasting, positive impact on the world. In *The Unstoppable Road to Wealth Creation*, we discussed how to achieve wealth, but it is equally important to understand that wealth can be a tool for contributing to the greater good. Wealth creation, when done right, allows individuals to impact their communities, the environment, and society as a whole. Giving with purpose not only enriches the lives of others but also creates a legacy that is far more meaningful than simply amassing financial resources.

In this chapter, we will explore how to balance wealth accumulation with purposeful philanthropy, emphasizing how financial success can be used to create positive change. Whether through charitable donations, impact investing, or social entrepreneurship, you'll learn how to use your wealth to create a ripple effect that improves the world for generations to come.

The Power of Purposeful Giving

Philanthropy is an essential aspect of wealth creation. However, there is a significant difference between giving for the sake of giving and giving with purpose. Wealthy individuals who give with purpose don't just donate money—they leverage their wealth, resources, and influence to drive tangible change. Giving with purpose is about aligning your wealth with your values and the causes that matter most to you.

In *The Things Wealthy People Do*, we explored how some of the wealthiest individuals in the world approach giving. They give with intention, aiming to leave a lasting impact rather than just making an occasional donation. Purpose-driven philanthropy is strategic, long-term, and highly impactful. Instead of treating philanthropy as a side activity, they integrate it into their broader life's work and goals. The goal is to create not only financial wealth but also social, environmental, and emotional wealth.

1. The Role of Charitable Donations

One of the most common methods of giving is through **charitable donations**. This type of philanthropy allows individuals to directly contribute to organizations and causes that align with their values. In *The Unstoppable Road to Wealth Creation*, we discussed how giving to charity can not only help those in need but also build a sense of fulfillment and purpose.

However, purposeful charitable donations are more than just giving money. It's about selecting the right causes and understanding the impact of your donation. Some of the wealthiest individuals focus their donations on **sustainable causes**—such as education, healthcare, poverty alleviation, or environmental conservation. Others choose to fund projects that aim to solve specific, systemic problems in society.

Example:

Consider Warren Buffett, one of the wealthiest men in the world. Through his **Giving Pledge**, he has committed to donating the majority of his wealth to charitable causes. Buffett's approach to giving is strategic, focusing on large-scale initiatives that can make a lasting difference. Rather than supporting every charitable cause, he chooses to focus on education, poverty alleviation, and health-related issues—areas where he feels his donation can create the most significant impact.

In *The Mind of a Trillionaire*, we learned that billionaires who give with purpose often take a hands-on approach in selecting the organizations they support. For instance, Bill Gates has been involved in **global health initiatives**, fighting diseases like malaria and polio. Through the **Bill and Melinda Gates Foundation**, Gates has driven a fundamental shift in how the world approaches health crises, leveraging his wealth to support sustainable solutions.

2. Impact Investing: Creating a Return Beyond Profit

In *The Things Wealthy People Do*, we discussed how wealth creation is not limited to the accumulation of financial assets. Investing with a social or environmental purpose, commonly referred to as **impact investing**, is another powerful tool for giving with purpose. Impact investing allows individuals to put their money into businesses or ventures that not only aim to provide a financial return but also generate positive social and environmental change.

Impact investing is an intentional strategy that aims to solve global challenges such as climate change, social inequality, and poverty. Unlike traditional investments that focus solely on profit, impact investments seek to create measurable positive impacts while still generating financial returns. These investments allow you to align your financial success with your values and contribute to the long-term well-being of society.

Example:

The **Billionaire's Impact Investment Funds**, such as those created by Richard Branson and the **Virgin Unite Foundation**, invest in initiatives focused on social change and sustainability. These funds are often directed toward clean energy, environmental protection, and poverty alleviation. By leveraging their wealth in this way, Branson and others ensure that their investments create both financial returns and a positive social impact.

Another example is **Patagonia**, a company known for its commitment to sustainability. The company's founder, Yvon Chouinard, has used **impact investing** to ensure that the business remains committed to environmental sustainability. Patagonia's profits are reinvested into efforts to preserve the planet, demonstrating that companies can be financially successful while also making a positive difference.

3. Social Entrepreneurship: Combining Business and Social Good

Social entrepreneurship is another compelling method for giving with purpose. Social entrepreneurs are individuals who use business principles to solve social, environmental, or cultural problems. This form of giving combines profit-making with a desire to make a lasting impact. In *The Mind of a Trillionaire*, we explored how wealthy individuals like Elon Musk and Richard Branson are using their business ventures to tackle global challenges such as climate change, space exploration, and renewable energy. These entrepreneurs have created businesses that solve real-world problems while creating wealth for their investors.

The advantage of social entrepreneurship lies in its sustainability. Unlike one-time donations, businesses that focus on social good have the potential to create ongoing positive impacts. By building businesses that align with social causes, entrepreneurs create jobs, provide services to underserved communities, and generate wealth that can be reinvested into further social initiatives.

Example:

TOMS Shoes is a prime example of social entrepreneurship. The company was founded on the idea of providing a pair of shoes to a child in need for every pair purchased. TOMS combines business success with social impact, creating jobs, boosting local economies, and improving the lives of children around the world. This innovative model of giving ensures that TOMS' impact continues to grow and expand, benefiting generations of children in need.

Another example is **Warby Parker**, a socially conscious eyewear company that provides free glasses to those in need for every pair sold. This model has turned the business of selling glasses into a force for good, demonstrating that even everyday businesses can make a meaningful difference.

4. The Psychological Benefits of Giving

In *The Unstoppable Road to Wealth Creation*, we discussed the idea that wealth is about more than just money—it's about fulfillment, purpose, and creating a legacy. Giving with purpose doesn't just benefit the recipient; it also benefits the giver. Philanthropy has been shown to have numerous psychological benefits, including increased happiness, a sense of purpose, and fulfillment.

Research shows that individuals who engage in giving are more likely to experience positive emotions, feel a sense of connection to others, and report higher life satisfaction. The act of giving can trigger the release of **endorphins** and other "feel-good" chemicals in the brain, leading to a positive cycle of generosity.

Example:

Consider the **Giving Pledge** that was established by Warren Buffett and Bill Gates, where billionaires pledge to give away at least half of their wealth during their lifetimes. For these individuals, the act of giving has become a source of joy and fulfillment, providing them with a sense of purpose beyond their business achievements.

5. The Long-Term Impact of Purposeful Giving

Giving with purpose is not just about immediate results—it's about creating lasting change. In *The Mind of a Trillionaire*, we examined how the wealthiest individuals focus on long-term goals rather than short-term gratification. Purposeful giving can create lasting social, economic, and environmental change that extends beyond an individual's lifetime.

One of the key aspects of purposeful giving is its ability to influence future generations. By creating sustainable initiatives, investing in education, and supporting projects that have long-term benefits, you ensure that your legacy will continue to impact the world long after you're gone.

Example:

The **Gates Foundation** focuses on long-term global health initiatives, working to eradicate diseases like polio and malaria. The foundation's commitment to addressing root causes and investing in sustainable solutions ensures that their efforts will continue to positively impact future generations.

Conclusion: The Ripple Effect of Purposeful Giving

Wealth can be an extraordinary tool for change. When combined with purpose, it has the power to transform communities, improve lives, and create lasting social and environmental progress. In *The Unstoppable Road to Wealth Creation*, we discussed the importance of using wealth as a vehicle for personal growth and empowerment. Now, we see how wealth can be used for the betterment of society, aligning financial success with a greater sense of purpose.

By embracing philanthropy, impact investing, and social entrepreneurship, you can ensure that your wealth continues to benefit others long after you've achieved personal success. Giving with purpose is about creating a legacy—one that is not just measured by financial wealth but by the positive impact it leaves on the world.

Chapter 18:

Becoming a Global Economic Influencer

In a rapidly evolving world where industries and societies are constantly shifting, the role of financial success extends far beyond personal wealth. Wealth is power, and those who master it can become influential in shaping not only their own destinies but the trajectory of global economies. The most successful individuals in the world are not just wealthy—they are powerful economic influencers who use their financial resources, networks, and platforms to drive systemic change across industries and societies.

In this chapter, we will explore how you can leverage your financial success to become a global economic influencer. Whether through impactful business ventures, innovative social initiatives, or even advocating for policy changes, you will learn how to use your wealth and influence to leave a lasting imprint on the world. The concepts of economic influence and how to strategically wield your power will be explored in depth, providing you with actionable steps to become a force for positive global change.

The Nature of Economic Influence

In *The Unstoppable Road to Wealth Creation*, we established that true financial success is not simply about accumulating wealth for personal enjoyment—it's about understanding how to use wealth to elevate your impact on the world. At its core, economic influence is the power to shape markets, industries, public opinion, and even governmental policies. Those who succeed in becoming economic influencers don't just make decisions based on personal gain; they make strategic moves that have ripple effects throughout the world.

Economic influencers can be entrepreneurs, philanthropists, activists, or thought leaders who use their resources and influence to create systemic change. Whether it's challenging established systems, spearheading innovative ideas, or creating platforms for social good, these individuals embody the power of wealth as a tool for transformation.

Understanding Your Unique Position as an Economic Influencer

To become an economic influencer, you must first understand your unique position in the economic landscape. In *The Mind of a Trillionaire*, we discussed how billionaires like Elon Musk and Jeff Bezos became more than just entrepreneurs—they became global economic forces. Their success didn't only stem from creating businesses; it arose from their ability to shape the future of industries like technology, space exploration, and renewable energy. These individuals leverage their financial power, vision, and networks to influence not just their companies but entire markets, shaping industries for generations to come.

In the same way, your unique position, skills, and expertise can be used to drive change, whether you're leading a global enterprise or advocating for broader systemic reforms.

Economic Influence Through Business Ventures

One of the primary ways to become an economic influencer is through your business ventures. As an entrepreneur, you have the ability to create businesses that drive economic change. Your business can have a profound impact on industries, consumer behavior, and even societal norms.

In *The Things Wealthy People Do*, we learned how successful businesspeople like Oprah Winfrey, Steve Jobs, and Mark Zuckerberg transformed not just their industries but society itself. Oprah leveraged her media empire to shift cultural narratives and address issues like personal empowerment, education, and equality. Steve Jobs revolutionized the tech industry, but his influence went further—Apple's products changed how people communicate, work, and engage with technology on a global scale.

Example: Consider the rise of **Tesla** under Elon Musk's leadership. Musk didn't simply start an electric car company—he created a movement. Tesla has played a major role in shifting the automotive industry toward sustainable energy, forcing legacy carmakers to rethink their entire business models. Beyond just selling electric vehicles, Musk's vision for

Tesla extends to energy solutions, creating a ripple effect that influences industries like energy production, battery storage, and even the future of transportation.

By creating or leading businesses that address large-scale global challenges, you can use your platform to shape industries and create meaningful change. Whether you're focused on innovation in technology, healthcare, green energy, or other sectors, your business venture can serve as a powerful catalyst for economic transformation.

Economic Influence Through Social Impact Initiatives

In addition to business ventures, many of the wealthiest and most influential individuals engage in social impact initiatives. By addressing societal issues such as poverty, education, healthcare, and climate change, these individuals use their financial resources to effect change at a global level.

We touched on the power of **philanthropy** in *The Unstoppable Road to Wealth Creation* and *The Things Wealthy People Do*. But social impact goes beyond traditional charity. Social entrepreneurship, impact investing, and large-scale social initiatives are powerful tools for driving global economic change.

Example: Consider the **Bill and Melinda Gates Foundation**. Bill Gates, through his foundation, has not only donated billions of dollars to global health and education but has also created initiatives that work to eradicate diseases, improve sanitation, and promote gender equality. His work has influenced global health policies, and the foundation has played a pivotal role in addressing critical global issues like malaria and polio.

Through social impact initiatives, you can combine your wealth with a commitment to positive change, using your influence to address global problems that affect entire populations. These initiatives often have the dual benefit of addressing critical social issues while also opening new markets and opportunities for businesses.

Economic Influence Through Policy Advocacy

Another significant way to become an economic influencer is through advocacy and policy reform. As your wealth and influence grow, you have the ability to push for systemic change through policy, legislation, and lobbying. While this may not be a path that many immediately consider, it is one that has immense power to shape global economies.

In *The Mind of a Trillionaire*, we discussed how **economic influencers** like Mark Zuckerberg and Bill Gates have influenced policy discussions in areas such as privacy, education, and healthcare. By leveraging their networks, resources, and expertise, they can bring attention to issues that shape not only industries but also national and global economic frameworks.

Example: George Soros, through his **Open Society Foundations**, has been a key player in advocating for democratic governance, human rights, and transparency in government. Soros uses his wealth to fund political activism and policy advocacy, supporting causes such as freedom of expression, anti-corruption measures, and global democracy. His influence has led to significant political reforms in various countries.

In the same vein, you can use your financial resources to advocate for policies that align with your economic goals and values. Whether it's advocating for environmental policies, pushing for regulatory reforms in your industry, or supporting education and healthcare policies, your influence can help shape the future of economies and industries.

Networking and Collaborating with Other Influencers

To amplify your economic influence, it's essential to build a network of other like-minded individuals, businesses, and organizations. Collaborating with other economic influencers—whether they're in business, politics, social entrepreneurship, or even academia—can magnify the impact you're able to achieve.

In *The Things Wealthy People Do*, we saw how some of the world's wealthiest individuals—such as Warren Buffett, Bill Gates, and Jeff Bezos—have leveraged their networks and collaborated with other industry leaders to drive positive global change. Through these partnerships, they have been able to tackle some of the world's biggest challenges, from climate change to poverty to global health.

Example: The **Giving Pledge** itself, which brings together some of the world's wealthiest individuals to pledge to give away at least half of their wealth, serves as an excellent example of the power of networking. By joining forces with others who share similar values, you can leverage your collective resources to create even greater global impact.

Building a Legacy of Economic Influence

Becoming a global economic influencer is not just about the impact you have today; it's also about the legacy you leave behind. In *The Unstoppable Road to Wealth Creation*, we discussed how important it is to think long-term and build a legacy of wealth. The same principle applies to becoming an economic influencer.

When you influence global economies and industries, your impact extends beyond your own lifetime. Whether through business ventures, philanthropic efforts, or policy reforms, your actions today can shape the future of industries, markets, and even societies. This is the power of **legacy influence**—the ability to leave a mark that transcends your own lifetime.

Conclusion: Becoming a Global Economic Influencer

Wealth is a powerful tool—one that can be used to shape the course of industries, societies, and entire global economies. By using your wealth strategically through business ventures, social impact initiatives, and policy advocacy, you can become a global economic influencer who drives meaningful change.

The key to becoming an economic influencer is understanding that true success isn't just about personal wealth—it's about using your wealth, influence, and resources to shape the world for the better. In *The Mind of a Trillionaire*, we saw how billionaires leverage their financial power to create lasting change. Similarly, you can use your resources to impact industries, communities, and the global economy, leaving behind a legacy of influence that shapes the world for generations to come.

Chapter 19:

Time vs. Money: The Ultimate Balance

Achieving financial freedom is a goal that many aspire to, but the true essence of financial freedom lies not just in accumulating wealth, but in achieving a harmonious balance between time and money. For most people, time and money are considered opposing forces—one is spent, while the other is earned. However, the key to truly unlocking financial success is in learning how to free up your time and use your resources efficiently to enjoy both financial security and a fulfilling lifestyle.

In this chapter, we will explore how to strike the ultimate balance between time and money. We'll look at the importance of building passive income streams, leveraging your financial resources, and delegating tasks effectively so that you can create more time for yourself. Whether you're an entrepreneur, an investor, or simply someone looking to improve their financial well-being, mastering this balance is essential to living the life you've always dreamed of.

The Relationship Between Time and Money

In *The Unstoppable Road to Wealth Creation*, we established that wealth accumulation isn't just about the hustle and grind—it's about making smart decisions that free up your time to focus on what truly matters. The relationship between time and money is a delicate one. The more time you spend working for money, the less time you have to enjoy it. On the other hand, the more you focus on generating passive income and managing your money wisely, the more time you free up to live the life you desire.

To understand this relationship fully, we need to look at the traditional approach to wealth: **trading time for money**. This is the model most people follow—working a job for a set wage, where the amount of money earned is directly tied to the amount of time worked. The problem with this approach is that there is an upper limit to how much time you can sell, and therefore, an upper limit to the amount of money you can earn.

In contrast, the wealthiest individuals have mastered the art of earning money without sacrificing their time. This is what we refer to as achieving **financial freedom**. By generating income from assets or businesses that operate independently of your time, you can enjoy a life of abundance without the constant pressure of work.

The Power of Passive Income

The concept of passive income is one of the most powerful tools for achieving the balance between time and money. In *The Things Wealthy People Do*, we explored how the world's wealthiest individuals use passive income streams to generate money without having to trade time for it. Passive income allows you to make money while you sleep, travel, or spend time with loved ones, providing you with the ultimate flexibility and freedom.

Passive income can come from various sources, such as:

- **Investments:** Dividends from stocks, interest from bonds, and capital gains from real estate or other investments are all examples of passive income streams. Once you've set up these income sources, they continue to generate revenue with minimal effort on your part.

- **Business Ventures:** By creating businesses that operate with minimal involvement from you—through automation, outsourcing, or a dedicated team—you can generate revenue without needing to be actively involved in every task. This is the hallmark of successful entrepreneurs who have mastered the art of delegation.

- **Royalties and Intellectual Property:** Another form of passive income is generating money from intellectual property such as books, music, patents, or digital products. As discussed in *The Mind of a Trillionaire*, authors, musicians, and inventors can earn royalties from their work long after the initial creation, allowing them to continue generating income while focusing on other ventures.

Example:

Consider the case of **Robert Kiyosaki**, author of *Rich Dad Poor Dad*. Kiyosaki has built an empire based on the principles of financial literacy, real estate investing, and entrepreneurship. His books and courses generate royalties, while his real estate investments produce passive income through rental properties. By setting up these income streams, Kiyosaki has created a model for achieving wealth that is not dependent on the hours he works.

The Importance of Delegating Tasks

Another crucial element of balancing time and money is **delegation**. As you scale your wealth and business, it becomes increasingly important to delegate tasks to others in order to focus on higher-level strategies. Wealthy individuals don't try to do everything themselves. Instead, they focus on their strengths and delegate tasks that are outside their core competencies.

In *The Unstoppable Road to Wealth Creation*, we highlighted how successful entrepreneurs and business owners build strong teams that handle the day-to-day operations of their businesses. By outsourcing tasks such as accounting, marketing, and customer service, they free up their time to focus on innovation, strategic planning, and growth.

Delegation is not just about hiring employees. It also involves leveraging technology and automation to reduce your workload. From accounting software to customer relationship management (CRM) systems, there are numerous tools available that can help you automate tasks and increase efficiency.

Example:

Take **Elon Musk**, whose many ventures—Tesla, SpaceX, and others—are highly successful because he delegates tasks to talented leaders and teams. He doesn't personally handle every aspect of the business. Instead, he focuses on the high-level vision, leaving the day-to-day operations to those who are best equipped to manage them.

Delegation also means hiring the right professionals to handle important aspects of your financial life, such as accountants, financial advisors, and legal experts. By relying on experts, you can ensure that your wealth is growing, protected, and optimized without spending your precious time on tasks that others can do more effectively.

Leveraging Technology to Save Time and Money

In *The Mind of a Trillionaire*, we explored how the most successful individuals use technology to maximize both their time and their wealth. Technology has drastically changed how we work, invest, and manage money. The right tools and systems can automate processes, provide valuable data insights, and allow you to make smarter, faster decisions.

For example, **investment apps** and **robo-advisors** are great tools for those who want to grow their wealth without spending hours researching stocks or managing their portfolios. These platforms can automatically invest your money based on your risk profile and financial goals, saving you time and effort.

Additionally, **automation tools** for business owners can streamline operations, manage customer interactions, and even handle social media marketing. By leveraging these technologies, you can create more time for high-value activities while still growing your business and wealth.

Example:

Richard Branson, founder of Virgin Group, has built a business empire by using technology to streamline operations. His ability to automate key aspects of his businesses, such as customer service and inventory management, has allowed him to focus on new ventures and expand his influence globally.

Balancing Time and Money: The Mindset of a Trillionaire

Becoming a global economic influencer, as discussed in *The Mind of a Trillionaire*, requires a shift in mindset. Wealthy individuals understand that their time is their most valuable asset. Rather than viewing time and money as opposing forces, they view time as an investment in their future.

In order to create lasting wealth and achieve true financial freedom, you must shift from thinking about trading time for money to thinking about creating systems and strategies that allow you to generate wealth independently of your time. By building passive income streams, delegating tasks, and using technology to your advantage, you can free up your time to enjoy life and pursue your passions.

Achieving the Balance

The ultimate balance between time and money comes from understanding that wealth creation is a marathon, not a sprint. By focusing on long-term goals and implementing the strategies outlined in this chapter—building passive income, delegating tasks, and leveraging technology—you can create a life where you have both financial success and the freedom to enjoy your time.

In *The Things Wealthy People Do*, we discussed the importance of maintaining a long-term vision and building systems that continue to grow wealth even when you're not actively working. Wealthy individuals know that the ultimate goal is not simply to accumulate wealth, but to create a life that allows them to enjoy both time and money in a fulfilling, meaningful way.

Conclusion

The balance between time and money is essential to achieving financial freedom and living a fulfilling life. By shifting your focus from trading time for money to building systems that allow you to earn while you sleep, delegate tasks, and leverage technology, you can create a lifestyle that enables you to enjoy both wealth and time. This balance is the key to unlocking your full potential and living the life you've always dreamed of.

Chapter 20:

Lifelong Wealth Mastery

Wealth mastery is not a destination but a lifelong pursuit. In a world where economic landscapes are constantly shifting, financial success requires more than just acquiring wealth; it demands an ongoing commitment to learning, adapting, and refining your strategies. The wealthy don't rest on their laurels after a few successes—they recognize that the true essence of wealth lies in the ability to sustain and grow it over time, continuously evolving with changing circumstances.

In this chapter, we will explore how to cultivate a mindset of wealth mastery, ensuring that your wealth continues to grow, evolve, and positively impact your life and the lives of others. Building on the lessons from *The Unstoppable Road to Wealth Creation*, *The Things Wealthy People Do*, and *The Mind of a Trillionaire*, we will examine the principles and practices that will help you maintain your financial success in the long run.

Understanding Wealth Mastery

Wealth mastery is more than just the ability to accumulate wealth. It's about cultivating the mindset and discipline needed to sustain financial success. In *The Unstoppable Road to Wealth Creation*, we established that wealth creation is a marathon, not a sprint. Mastery, therefore, requires patience, foresight, and a commitment to continuous improvement.

Achieving wealth is often seen as a goal in itself, but mastering wealth means taking a holistic approach—balancing accumulation with responsible management, protection, and growth. It's about being able to weather the inevitable storms of life and finance, always staying the course despite challenges. Just as *The Mind of a Trillionaire* explains, mastering wealth is about shaping your own destiny and not relying solely on external factors like luck or market trends.

Wealth mastery requires more than good fortune or short-term gains; it's about cultivating a set of principles that guide your decision-making in both prosperous and lean times. This involves adapting to changing circumstances, reevaluating strategies, and continually learning and growing as a wealth creator.

Lifelong Learning: The Foundation of Wealth Mastery

One of the most critical components of wealth mastery is the commitment to lifelong learning. In *The Things Wealthy People Do*, we discussed how wealthy individuals prioritize education and personal growth. This mindset is not only about formal education but also about learning from experiences, mistakes, and successes.

The richest individuals continuously evolve by seeking new knowledge. They read books, attend seminars, and hire mentors to guide them. But the key is not just gathering information—it's the ability to apply that knowledge effectively to achieve long-term financial success.

Example:

Take the example of **Warren Buffet**, one of the world's wealthiest investors. Buffett is known for his love of reading, spending up to 80% of his day reading books, reports, and other educational materials. He is a firm believer in continuous learning, constantly refining his investment strategies. His dedication to lifelong learning has been one of the cornerstones of his wealth-building success.

To master wealth, you must always be open to new ideas and approaches. This requires a mindset that is adaptable, willing to accept that the strategies that worked in the past may need to be adjusted or refined in the future. The financial world is ever-evolving, and staying current with trends, tools, and strategies is essential for sustaining wealth.

The Importance of Reflection

Learning isn't just about acquiring new knowledge; it's also about reflecting on past experiences. As discussed in *The Unstoppable Road to Wealth Creation*, reflection allows you to understand what has worked for you and what hasn't, making it possible to adjust your approach and improve your wealth-building strategies.

Reflection is essential in wealth mastery because it helps you avoid repeating mistakes and capitalize on your successes. Regularly taking time to assess your goals, financial strategies, and outcomes will help you maintain a clear vision and stay focused on your long-term financial objectives.

Example:

The late **Steve Jobs** was known for his ability to reflect on his past ventures, learning from both his successes and failures. Jobs famously returned to Apple after being ousted from the company, bringing with him the insights gained from his earlier ventures. His ability to adapt and reflect helped Apple become one of the most valuable companies in the world.

Building Financial Resilience

In the journey of wealth mastery, resilience is key. Life will always present challenges, whether they come in the form of economic downturns, personal setbacks, or unforeseen circumstances. The richest individuals are not immune to these challenges, but they are often better equipped to deal with them.

In *The Mind of a Trillionaire*, we explored how the wealthiest individuals respond to adversity. Instead of panicking, they focus on solutions, leveraging their knowledge, networks, and resources to navigate through tough times. Wealth mastery involves building resilience by preparing for the unexpected, creating contingency plans, and ensuring that your financial foundation is strong enough to weather economic storms.

Example:

When the **2008 financial crisis** hit, many companies and individuals experienced significant losses. However, some of the wealthiest individuals, like **Elon Musk**, managed to weather the storm by remaining focused on their long-term vision. Musk was able to keep Tesla and SpaceX afloat by securing strategic investments and continuing to innovate, despite the challenges that came with the economic downturn.

Building a Legacy Through Wealth Mastery

In wealth mastery, it's essential to think beyond your own financial goals and focus on the legacy you want to leave. In *The Unstoppable Road to Wealth Creation*, we highlighted how creating generational wealth can change the trajectory of your family's future. However, wealth mastery isn't just about accumulating wealth for the next generation—it's about teaching the next generation how to manage and sustain that wealth.

Wealth mastery involves creating systems that ensure your assets are protected, preserved, and grown across generations. This could include setting up trusts, estate planning, and educating your family about financial literacy.

Example:

Bill and Melinda Gates have established the **Gates Foundation**, using their wealth to address global health and poverty issues. Through their philanthropy, they've created a legacy that extends far beyond their own financial success. Their foundation is designed not only to help others but to inspire future generations to use wealth for social good.

Wealth Mastery Through Strategic Action

While mindset and learning are crucial to wealth mastery, it's the ability to take strategic action that separates the successful from the merely wealthy. In *The Things Wealthy People Do*, we discussed how the wealthy are intentional with their actions, focusing on investments, business opportunities, and financial strategies that align with their long-term goals.

Wealth mastery requires making bold, informed decisions and taking consistent, calculated risks. It's not about relying on luck but about making strategic moves that align with your goals. By following a well-thought-out plan and continually reassessing your strategies, you ensure that your wealth continues to grow and evolve.

Leveraging the Power of Networks

Another key to wealth mastery is leveraging the power of networks. Wealthy individuals understand the importance of surrounding themselves with like-minded, successful individuals. In *The Mind of a Trillionaire*, we explored how the wealthiest people have a network of advisors, mentors, and business partners who help them stay ahead of the curve and make smarter decisions.

Building a strong network is essential for sharing knowledge, discovering new opportunities, and gaining the support you need to navigate challenges. Your network can open doors to investment opportunities, business ventures, and collaborations that can accelerate your wealth-building journey.

Example:

Oprah Winfrey is a prime example of how powerful networks can influence wealth mastery. Over the years, she has surrounded herself with trusted advisors and collaborators who have helped her grow her business empire. Her network has been instrumental in her ability to evolve and stay relevant in an ever-changing media landscape.

Conclusion

Wealth mastery is not about getting rich quickly or achieving success through shortcuts. It is about understanding that wealth is a lifelong pursuit, requiring dedication, discipline, and continuous learning. By reflecting on your experiences, building resilience, and focusing on strategic action, you can cultivate a mindset that sustains financial greatness for the long term.

As you continue to learn, adapt, and refine your wealth-building strategies, you will not only grow your financial resources but also make a lasting impact on your own life and the lives of others. Wealth mastery is about creating a legacy that transcends your own success—leaving a mark on the world and paving the way for future generations to thrive.

Chapter 21:

Activating Your Financial DNA

In the journey to financial greatness, it's easy to get lost in the noise of endless strategies, theories, and advice. Many people are eager to learn how to create wealth, but without a clear blueprint and personal commitment, all the knowledge in the world remains theoretical. This final chapter is designed to guide you in applying the wealth-building strategies discussed throughout this book, helping you activate your financial DNA and take immediate action toward your financial goals.

Just like a blueprint defines the structure of a building, your financial DNA provides the foundation for your wealth-building journey. By unlocking and harnessing the power of your unique financial traits, you can create lasting success, overcome obstacles, and confidently pursue the life and legacy you desire. This is your roadmap for creating the life of your dreams and achieving financial freedom.

Understanding Financial DNA

Before diving into how to activate your financial DNA, it's crucial to understand what this concept entails. Your financial DNA refers to the unique set of beliefs, habits, behaviors, and thought patterns that shape your approach to money. Much like genetic DNA dictates physical traits, your financial DNA shapes how you handle money, wealth-building, and investment opportunities. However, unlike genetic DNA, financial DNA can be molded, enhanced, and transformed with conscious effort.

In *The Unstoppable Road to Wealth Creation*, we discussed the importance of mindset in financial success. Your mindset forms the core of your financial DNA. If you want to achieve long-term wealth, you must first understand your financial habits and beliefs. This chapter will delve deeper into how you can actively reprogram your financial DNA to align with your wealth-building aspirations.

The Power of Your Financial Mindset

To activate your financial DNA, it all begins with transforming your mindset. Everything you do with money is influenced by how you think about it. If you perceive money as scarce or something to be feared, your decisions and actions will align with that belief, leading to a cycle of missed opportunities and financial limitations. On the other hand, if you view money as a tool for creating opportunities, building legacy, and achieving freedom, your actions will reflect that, ultimately leading to prosperity.

In *The Mind of a Trillionaire*, we explored how the wealthiest individuals view money. They understand that wealth is not just about accumulating material possessions but about creating freedom and opportunity—not just for themselves, but for others as well. This shift in perspective is crucial when activating your financial DNA. The wealthiest people have learned to see money as a tool for growth, expansion, and transformation.

Example:

Elon Musk is an excellent example of someone who has embraced the power of mindset. Musk was not driven by the pursuit of money for its own sake. Instead, his primary focus was always innovation, creating solutions for the world's most pressing problems. His mindset shifted away from simply accumulating wealth to creating lasting, transformative change through his companies like Tesla and SpaceX.

To activate your financial DNA, start by shifting your mindset toward abundance and growth. Instead of fearing financial risks or worrying about scarcity, embrace the idea that opportunities for wealth creation are everywhere—and they are yours to claim. Wealth is not a finite resource, but a constantly expanding opportunity. This belief alone will set you on the right path.

Establishing Your Financial Goals

Once your mindset is in place, the next step in activating your financial DNA is setting clear, actionable financial goals. Goals give you direction and purpose, providing a concrete roadmap for your wealth-building journey. In *The Unstoppable Road to Wealth Creation*, we discussed the importance of setting both short-term and long-term financial goals, as these act as your compass, helping you navigate the complexities of wealth-building.

However, not all goals are created equal. To activate your financial DNA, your goals must be specific, measurable, attainable, relevant, and time-bound (SMART). These criteria ensure that your goals are not just vague aspirations, but actionable steps that move you closer to your desired financial future.

Example:

Let's say your goal is to achieve financial freedom within ten years. A SMART goal might look like: "I will save and invest 20% of my monthly income in a diversified portfolio of stocks, bonds, and real estate to reach a net worth of $5 million by 2035." This goal is clear, measurable, and has a specific timeframe.

Developing a Wealth Strategy

With your mindset aligned and your goals set, the next step in activating your financial DNA is developing a wealth strategy. In *The Things Wealthy People Do*, we explored the idea of the wealthy acting with purpose and intention in their financial decisions. Wealthy individuals don't stumble upon success; they create it with deliberate, strategic actions.

Creating a wealth strategy is about understanding where your money should go, how it should be allocated, and what steps you need to take to grow it. It involves understanding investment options, debt management, passive income generation, and more.

Your strategy should include:

1. **Investment Plans:** Allocate a portion of your wealth to investments that align with your long-term goals, whether it's stocks, real estate, or businesses.

2. **Income Streams:** Look at ways to diversify your income—through business ventures, side hustles, or investments. Passive

income, such as rental income or dividends, can provide the financial freedom you desire.

3. **Debt Management:** Develop a plan for eliminating high-interest debt and leveraging low-interest debt to grow your wealth.

4. **Financial Education:** Commit to learning about new investment opportunities and staying informed about market trends. Wealthy individuals consistently educate themselves about emerging markets and financial strategies.

Example:

A practical illustration of this is **Robert Kiyosaki**, author of *Rich Dad Poor Dad*, who advocates for investing in assets that generate passive income. His strategy is based on acquiring real estate properties, starting businesses, and investing in stocks that produce steady returns. By following this strategy, Kiyosaki was able to achieve financial freedom and build substantial wealth.

In order to activate your financial DNA, you must devise your own wealth strategy. Consider your current financial situation and where you want to be in the next five, ten, or twenty years. Then, design a strategy that aligns with your goals, taking into account your risk tolerance, current resources, and time frame.

Taking Action and Overcoming Fear

The most important part of activating your financial DNA is action. Knowledge and planning are important, but without execution, they are meaningless. One of the greatest obstacles to taking action is fear—the fear of making mistakes, losing money, or failing to achieve your goals. In *The Mind of a Trillionaire*, we discussed how the wealthiest individuals are not afraid of failure. Instead, they view mistakes as opportunities for learning and growth.

Fear often paralyzes people from taking the first step toward their financial goals. But the reality is that in order to activate your financial DNA, you must take calculated risks and embrace the possibility of failure. Every successful wealth creator has faced setbacks, but their ability to take action despite those setbacks is what has led them to long-term success.

Example:

Consider **Richard Branson**, founder of the Virgin Group. Branson has faced numerous setbacks in his career, including failed ventures and business collapses. However, his willingness to take risks, coupled with his ability to learn from failure, has allowed him to build an empire across multiple industries. Branson's story is a testament to the power of taking action, even in the face of fear and uncertainty.

Building Your Financial Legacy

Finally, as you activate your financial DNA, it's crucial to think about the legacy you want to leave behind. Wealth-building is not just about personal gain—it's about creating something that lasts. In *The Unstoppable Road to Wealth Creation*, we discussed the importance of planning for generational wealth. This involves not just accumulating assets, but also ensuring that your financial success benefits future generations.

To build a legacy, consider ways in which your wealth can serve others. This might involve creating family trusts, making charitable donations, or investing in businesses or causes that align with your values. Legacy-building is about leaving a positive impact, both financially and socially, that extends far beyond your lifetime.

Example:

Warren Buffett has pledged to give away 99% of his fortune to charity, ensuring that his wealth will continue to benefit others long after his passing. Buffett's commitment to philanthropy is an integral part of his legacy, and his approach to wealth creation reflects his belief that wealth should serve the greater good.

Conclusion

Activating your financial DNA is the key to unlocking your wealth-building potential. By shifting your mindset, setting clear goals, developing a strategic plan, taking action, and building a lasting legacy, you can create a life of financial freedom and prosperity. Wealth mastery is not about luck or chance—it's about taking deliberate, strategic action with a clear vision of your future.

As you implement the principles from *The Unstoppable Road to Wealth Creation*, *The Things Wealthy People Do*, and *The Mind of a Trillionaire*, remember that the true power lies within you. Your financial DNA is yours to activate, and by doing so, you can shape your own destiny and build the life of your dreams.

Bonus Chapters:

Building Wealth Beyond Money

Bonus Chapter 22:

Using Relationships to Build Wealth

Introduction: Achieving financial success often requires collaboration with others. This chapter discusses how to utilize your relationships—whether with mentors, business partners, or peers—to build wealth and open doors to new opportunities. By nurturing a strong network, you can accelerate your financial journey, gain invaluable advice, and create successful ventures.

The Influence of Networking: Networking is more than just exchanging contact details; it's about forming meaningful relationships with people who can help propel you toward your goals. In *The Unstoppable Road to Wealth Creation*, we explored how networking can fuel your career and business growth. Whether it's investors, advisors, or collaborators, everyone you meet can play a pivotal role in your financial success.

Example:

Consider **Oprah Winfrey**—her immense success isn't just the result of her talent, but also the relationships she cultivated with influential figures in media, business, and philanthropy. By surrounding herself with strategic allies, Oprah grew her ventures into highly profitable enterprises, demonstrating the importance of building strong, supportive relationships in your own wealth-building efforts.

Building Strong Partnerships: Strategic partnerships are essential for business success. In *The Things Wealthy People Do*, we delved into how the wealthiest individuals team up with the right people to create and scale businesses. Finding the right partners who complement your strengths can propel your success. But it's crucial to choose partners wisely—ensure your values and visions align to minimize friction and maximize synergy.

Example:

Think of **Bill Gates** and **Paul Allen**—their partnership in founding Microsoft was a crucial part of the company's rise. Gates brought the strategic vision, while Allen contributed technical expertise. Their complementary skills made the collaboration highly effective and led to Microsoft's dominance in the tech world.

Seeking Mentorship: Learning from others is a key component of success. Wealthy individuals surround themselves with experienced mentors and advisors who offer wisdom and guidance during critical decision-making moments. In *The Mind of a Trillionaire*, we talked about how continuous learning and mentorship can accelerate your journey to wealth.

Example:

Mark Zuckerberg sought guidance from **Steve Jobs** when founding Facebook. Jobs mentored Zuckerberg on leadership, product development, and business strategy. Zuckerberg's willingness to learn from someone who had already achieved massive success was pivotal in Facebook's growth.

Conclusion: Building wealth isn't a solitary pursuit. By leveraging your network, forming valuable partnerships, and seeking mentorship, you open yourself up to a world of opportunities that accelerate your journey toward financial success. Remember, wealth is not just about accumulating money—it's about the people you connect with and the lessons you learn along the way.

Bonus Chapter 23:

The Importance of Health in Wealth Creation

Introduction: Wealth creation is not just about financial accumulation—it also requires maintaining physical, mental, and emotional health. This chapter examines how personal well-being plays a critical role in achieving long-term financial success. A strong body and mind are essential to sustaining the energy, focus, and resilience needed to build lasting wealth.

The Link Between Health and Wealth: The pursuit of wealth demands hard work and dedication, but it is impossible to achieve success if you don't have the vitality to keep going. In *The Unstoppable Road to Wealth Creation*, we emphasized the importance of discipline in achieving financial goals. That same discipline should apply to maintaining your health, as staying physically and mentally fit enhances productivity, clarity, and decision-making ability—key elements in financial success.

Physical Health: Physical fitness is an important part of achieving success. Wealthy individuals recognize that their health is their most valuable asset, and without good health, everything else falls apart. Regular exercise, proper nutrition, and adequate rest are vital for maintaining energy and focus. In *The Things Wealthy People Do*, we discussed how many successful individuals incorporate fitness into their daily routines to stay sharp and energized.

Example:

Richard Branson, the founder of Virgin Group, attributes much of his success to maintaining a daily exercise routine. Whether it's swimming, cycling, or hiking, Branson's commitment to physical health has allowed him to run his empire with sustained energy and clarity.

Mental and Emotional Well-being: In *The Mind of a Trillionaire*, we explored how wealth creators maintain emotional and mental clarity despite the pressures they face. Mental health is as critical as physical health for anyone striving for success. Stress, burnout, and anxiety can derail your financial plans, so developing emotional resilience and maintaining mental well-being is crucial for sustained success.

Example:

Oprah Winfrey advocates for the importance of mental well-being, often discussing how she practices meditation and therapy to maintain emotional balance. Her commitment to mental health has allowed her to handle the pressures of running a global media empire while maintaining a sense of purpose.

Investing in Health: Wealthy individuals view health as an investment. They understand that spending on fitness, healthcare, and self-care is essential to maintaining long-term productivity and focus. Whether it's hiring a personal trainer, following a nutritious diet, or regularly checking in with a healthcare professional, they prioritize their health as a core element of their success strategy.

Conclusion: As you pursue financial greatness, don't overlook the importance of maintaining your health. A healthy body and mind provide the foundation for success, ensuring you have the stamina and clarity to execute your wealth-building strategies. Wealth isn't just about financial freedom—it's about living a balanced life where you can enjoy your success and well-being simultaneously. Invest in your health now, and it will yield great returns in your journey to lasting financial success.

THE END!